FROM TINKERING TO
TORQUING

A BEGINNER'S GUIDE
TO **TRACTORS** AND **TOOLS**

FROM TINKERING TO
TORQUING
A BEGINNER'S GUIDE
TO **TRACTORS** AND **TOOLS**

ROGER
WELSCH

MBI

DEDICATION

For good ol' Verne Holoubek...

First published in 2005 by MBI, an imprint of MBI Publishing Company, Galtier Plaza, Suite 200, 380 Jackson Street, St. Paul, MN 55101-3885 USA

MBI titles are also available at discounts in bulk quantity for industrial or sales-promotional use. For details write to Special Sales Manager at MBI Publishing Company, Galtier Plaza, Suite 200, 380 Jackson Street, St. Paul, MN 55101-3885 USA.

ISBN-13: 978-0-7603-2082-2
ISBN-10: 0-7603-2082-9

Editor: Darwin Holmstrom
Designer: Brenda Canales
Cover Design: Rochelle Schultz

Printed in the United States of America

On the cover: Roger and his wife Linda, who obviously shares the guttural pleasure Rog receives from restoring old tractors. All wives do, you know. *Lee Klancher*

CONTENTS

A PREFACE TO A FOREWORD FROM DAVE MOWITZ, MACHINERY EDITOR, *SUCCESSFUL FARMING* MAGAZINE, AND FOUNDER OF AGELESS IRON

Dave Mowitz is not only a farm boy, a lifelong agriculturist, a talented writer, and a friend to all of us who love tractors and tools; he is in many ways the Patron Saint of Ageless Iron. It was Dave's work in *Successful Farming's Ageless Iron* that introduced me to the world of rust, dirt, pain, tractors, farm implements, and creative language. I remember the precise moment I walked into the Dannebrog tavern and saw a bunch of my cronies bent over a tattered copy of a tear sheet from *Successful Farming*—admiring, arguing, wondering. I borrowed those few pages and wrote to Dave for advice about possibly doing some writing about my own experiences. My connection to Dave then led me to a long and warm association with MBI Publishing, the premier publisher for those of us who love tractors and tractor people.

I am grateful to Dave Mowitz for many things. At this moment, I thank him for taking the time and trouble in his unbelievably busy schedule to offer up the following words of wisdom to those of you who are new to this world in which he and I are now venerable elders.

As for the last request he makes to me in the words below—Dave, by now you should know that the formulas for working with antique tractor magnetos all start the same way: "Eye of newt, and toe of frog, wool of bat and tongue of dog. . . ."

A Foreword from Dave Mowitz, Machinery Editor, *Successful Farming* Magazine, and Founder of Ageless Iron

Anyone who has had to assemble a Christmas toy, set a VCR, or prime a diesel-injector pump has come to either curse or appreciate the craft of technical writing. A case in point is my recent ordeal of erecting a jungle gym. The task seemed simple enough—four legs, a crossbeam, swings, and a slide. Put 'em together. There you are . . . a jungle gym.

Mind you, as a farm boy, I can operate a 200-plus-horsepower diesel powering a 300-plus-foot-deep turbine well pumping 1,000 gallons of water a minute to an electrically driven center-pivot sprinkler with a control board that looked like something utilized to launch satellites from Cape Kennedy. Confident, I told my wife, "A jungle gym? No sweat! Should have it up and running in a couple of hours."

A day later I came to realize that the author of the gym's so-called installation instructions left a few things unsaid. For example, the support legs were crimped in such a way that if they were not inserted properly—and in a certain particular order—the resulting structure's legs would splay out like those of a dead cow left in a sunny pasture for three days in the middle of July.

The jungle gym reminds me of another time when a fun-loving veterinarian instructed me, little Davey Mowitz, in the fine art of inserting a trocar (a 1-inch-diameter stainless-steel tube with a surgically sharp point at one end) into the belly of a dead, bloated animal. I won't trouble you with the unsavory details except that the vet gave me painfully detailed instructions on how to insert the device. Following those directions to the letter, I succeeded in deflating the beast with effects that can only be described as spectacular. Later I was told by friends with less cruel senses of humor that a 10-foot pole with a sharpened point can be used with similar effect while avoiding the nasty results of this operation.

Ahhhh, practical jokes on the farm! The point is, if we weren't well enough equipped as it is to make our own mistakes, it seems there are always plenty of "experts" around who are perfectly willing to give the green beginner even more unfortunate experiences to draw upon in the learning process. As almost every beginner in almost any endeavor will find out soon enough, the real trick is to find an expert who has a sense of humor, but who is also willing to pass along the lessons without covering the pathetic newcomer with a generous coating of whatever is inside the cow.

I need to get to the point here, which is that almost anyone with the knowledge can give clear verbal directions on how, for example, to adjust a carburetor. But will the directions from an expert be clear enough for the beginner to understand? And interesting enough to listen to? And innocent enough that the poor beginner doesn't come away from the seminar with second-degree burns and a hernia? Turning information into a clearly understood, interesting written guide that anyone can follow is a true gift. And Rog has that gift.

To be perfectly honest, I was somewhat dubious of Roger's abilities to tackle the technical aspects of antique tractor ownership and restoration. Mind you, Rog is a wordsmith of enormous talent who has authored no less than 32 books. His verse is so well crafted that words often leap off the page and echo in your head as if you had just finished a personal conversation with the man. Certainly ol' Rog's humorous insights into the human condition are legendary. His raucous literary celebrations of the tractor as a metaphor for life mark him as the poet laureate of antique tractor collectors. Truly, through Roger's eyes, we have discovered the antique tractor's common beauty.

Roger is no stranger to the subject of mechanicking. His rural tractor shop stands as dramatic testimony to his personal relationship with nuts, valves, pistons, and gears. A mighty wonder of tools line the shop's walls. The floor has taken on the deep patina of oil, axle grease, and solvent (as, I might note, has Rog himself). Rags, rust, and spare parts litter the work-benches of this mechanical sanctuary.

Roger warns in the first chapter of this book that it is "not an encyclopedia, or manual, or even an introduction to tractor restoration, repair, or mechanicking." Yet this book comes as close to any guide I've ever read in outlining the technical heart of the hobby. The following pages are written in such a way that even a beginning collector with no idea how a transmission works will complete this guide mechanically enriched and with a solid basis upon which to at least converse with the experts without sounding like a complete idiot. Even grizzled old historic-horsepower gurus will garner valuable information, good memories, and certainly some laughs from the following pages. Hats off to you, Rog. Even I understood and relished every page, and that's saying something because I thought I had seen everything by now.

Oh, by the way, since you have mastered the art of describing the impossibly complicated in a simple, interesting, clear, and amusing way, would you mind sending me instructions on how to set the magneto on my Deere B?

[A note from the author: Thanks for the good words, Dave. Sure, of course I'd be glad to help out an old buddy with a problem as simple as this. The answer is on page 111, plain as can be.]

ACKNOWLEDGMENTS

Before we launch off into the wacky world of old tractors, I want to thank some of the people who have been so helpful to me, not just with this book but with so many other projects in the past. Everyone should have a friend like Dick Day. He's a great friend and a guy who knows a lot about a lot of things. He has helped me out again and again over the years with everything from tractors and tools to my work as a writer. In fact, Dick proofread this manuscript, so if you find anything at all wrong—besides the four errors I put in here on purpose—then it's Dick's fault. As if Dick weren't already lucky enough to have a buddy like me, he also has a perfectly wonderful wife, Deb, who not only tolerates him and his friends, but who also proofed these pages without me even asking. I think maybe she just wanted to check on what it is us guys talk about. But whatever the reason, Deb, thank you very much for your careful reading.

Writing is a lonely way to make a living, and while a lot of people may read and appreciate a book, not many take the time to contact the author personally and express support. Well, Steve Manzer of Manzer Implement in Osmond, Nebraska, is a guy who does, and in a big way. I have learned a lot from Steve about the world of *new* tractors. He has been helpful in finding parts for *old* tractors, and he and the people at AGCO have supported my work in ways that make me wonder if maybe someone hasn't made a big mistake along the way, and sooner or later I'm going to be found out!

Gene Lorang, Melvin Nelson, Melvin Halsey, Dennis Adams, Dan Selden, Kenny Porath, and Al Schmitt have been good friends through all sorts of crazy projects, of which old tractors are not the least. Paul Jensen, Big Kahuna of Jensales tractor manuals and other tractor-oriented publications, has been a source of information, publications, and lots of laughs over the years, and I thank him for that. (If you are looking for any sort of manual reprints and reproductions for old tractors of any sort, I strongly recommend that you check with Paul at Jensales, 200 Main Street, Manchester, Minnesota 56007, 1-507-826-3666 or www.jensales.com)

Last, but certainly not least, I must again acknowledge the immense contribution to my work by my beloved partner in all things, Lovely Linda. I don't want to get all mushy here but dang, I sure have been lucky in this life to win a prize like her along the line. On a daily basis, I pray she never figures out what an uneven bargain this is.

INTRODUCTION

I have jokingly suggested that it is a real mistake to write a book about a subject you know a lot about. That kind of restriction really cramps your opportunities to write other books, if you think about it. I mean jeez, how many areas are you an expert in? One? Two? At the most three? Nope, I recommend writing about something you know absolutely nothing about. After all, how many things do you know nothing about? Hundreds? Maybe thousands?! Possibly *millions*! Think about it—heart transplants, burying beetles, ocean algae, Inuit sled construction, meteor impact crystal forms . . . The list goes on and on. What's more, when you write as an expert, everyone feels free to snipe at you every time you make some little, minor mistake. If you admit right up front that you know absolutely nothing about what you are writing, you leave the carpers and whiners not so much as the tiniest toehold to start their efforts to tear you down.

Well, this time I'm going to fly into the face of all my well-intentioned and flawless logic. This is a book about one of the few things I know plenty about—what it's like to be a newcomer to the world of antique tractors, mechanicking, shop equipment, tools, engines, and transmissions. Originally I thought this would be a book for young readers, kids who were about to be lured into the world of smoky shops and rusting parts by loving parents, grandparents, and uncles. And to some extent it still is. That's where my heart is, heaven knows. I'm not really optimistic about the direction our world seems to be moving, or what it is doing to our children. Which means I don't much like the children of this New Age. They are snotty, arrogant, not very bright, lazy, greedy, inconsiderate, rude, loud mouthed, and, well, make your own list.

But as I wrote in the last chapter of *Old Tractors and the Men Who Love Them*, I have had that curmudgeonly attitude considerably modified by the young people I have encountered in the decade I have been writing about old tractors. The kids I have met who are enthusiastic about old tractors also seem to have a respect for old coots who love old tractors. Since that book came out, and to some degree because that book came out, I have made some real friends with youngsters who have an interest in antique machinery. So I would like to save America and the world by dragging more young minds into the tractor shop. Maybe this book can ease the way for that miracle.

Then I got to thinking, *Hey, maybe I should consider helping other people understand what's going on with us nut cases who bang on rusty iron, belabor stuck parts, and scrounge around in junkyards full of battered and broken tractors.* And I thought about my own Lovely Linda. She has no intentions whatsoever of joining me out in my smoky, loud, stinky shop—in fact, that's why I like to keep it a touch smoky, loud, and stinky. But she might like to know more about what my friends and I are talking about when we discuss ridge reaming, cylinder pulling, and seal pulling.

Okay, I'll admit that my intentions are not always charitable and generous. There's something in this for me too. I once spent a day in the shop working on an old tractor and the next morning took off on a 200-mile trip. I stopped along the way to get some gas and was stunned as I stepped out of the car to find that the temperature had plummeted 40 degrees. I almost froze as I stood there by the pump holding the nozzle into my gas tank. I paid my bill, got back into the warm car, and continued my drive.

Then a dreadful thought popped into my head: I had left the tractor I was working on sitting in my shop, heated only by a wood stove. I imagined the temperature plunging in the shop as the fire in my stove burned down and eventually out, until the inside of that shop was as cold as the wind whistling around me while I zipped down the highway. I had left water in the radiator and block of that tractor. As that water froze, it was certain to wreck the radiator and maybe even the engine block as it froze solid.

But what could I do about this impending, certain disaster? My mind whirred through a list of possibilities. Turn around and drive three hours back? Nah, can't do that. Call my friends and turn them loose in my tool-filled shop to take an inventory of my shop tools and equipment after they spent two minutes draining the engine and radiator? That would be even more expensive than replacing the parts. Should I call Linda and ask her to turn the drain plugs and drain out that water?

Hmmm . . . Call Linda and ask her to turn the drain plugs and drain out that water . . . Linda barely knows how to get into my shop. I imagine she knows where the front of a tractor is, but if I tell her to open the drains on both the block and the bottom of the radiator, would she even know where to look for the block, much less the radiator? Would she know what a drain plug looks like? Or how to turn it open? How would I explain over the telephone from a moving car the basic mechanic's rule: "Rightie tightie, leftie loosie?"

I had no choice. I was going to have to call Linda and give her a long-distance lesson in tractor cooling systems. And then ask her to go out into the dark, dirty shop and grope around for the drain plugs, describing in words alone—no twisting around with my fingers and waving of arms—where to look, what to do, what *not* to do. All this seemed like a fool's errand, and yet I simply could not imagine an alternative plan.

I called Linda. I told her as much as I could: Stand in front of the tractor and look right (no, your right). Down at the bottom of the radiator and the side of the engine, you'll see two little doohickeys that have ears on them, like a plug with rounded wings sticking out. Turn them counterclockwise. Watch for water to start running out . . . that's good. Now open the drain plug wide open—no, it won't hurt if the plugs fall out—and let the water run out onto the floor. Use a bucket if you can find one. If the plugs are stuck, find some pliers on the workbench and . . . no offense, my dear, but do you know what pliers look like? It was a serious question.

I hung up the telephone and drove on into the night, imagining Linda wading through the snow out to the shop, trying to find a light, hoping those plugs weren't stuck or turned too tight. I drove and waited. I anticipated an anguished call, maybe with minor injuries from when she kicked a jack stand or cut herself on the radiator shield. I dreaded the tears that were sure to flow when she couldn't find the plugs or turn them. I tried to think of what steps I could take next to save the engine and radiator when this errand I sent her on failed, as it almost certainly would.

My car phone rang. I answered. It was Linda. I held my breath. "Hi, honey. I'm sorry to do this to you," I said. "I just didn't see anything else I could do. I understand if you couldn't bring this one off, and—"

"Done," she said.

"Done?"

"Yep, turned out both plugs, drained the tractor, closed the shop back up."

Well, now I had another problem, of course. If I didn't already owe this woman big-time for simply marrying me and sticking with me so many years, this was now going to cost me not just a dinner and some kind of gooey movie with two women talking endlessly about their relationships—not a single car chase or explosion; now my debt had suddenly risen to include things like new furniture for the front room, redecorating the kitchen, and maybe even shaving every day for a year.

Still, I was grateful. No matter what it was going to cost me, Linda had entered an area where she had almost complete ignorance, learned instantly and remotely the barest kind of information, and had saved my sorry rear end from an error of my own making. If she could perform a rescue like that for me, knowing almost nothing about old tractors, I began thinking, what might she be able to save me from if she had the most basic, barest information about tractors, tools, and the shop?

Clearly, I could save a lot of tractor mechanics a lot of trouble if I wrote a book they could give to their children for Christmas instead of something silly like a mountain bike or trip to Disneyland. They could give a copy to their spouses instead of wastefully spending money on a cruise to the Caribbean or a new Lexus convertible. So, this book is not just for kids who want some basic information so they can start a lifetime of restoring old tractors, but for friends and spouses who want some idea what the heck is going on out there in the shop, or who are sent out there on a snowy, dark night to turn a plug and earn themselves some mighty big rewards for their efforts.

But that's not the sum total of my intentions here, either. This book is for people like me too. That's why I am an expert in this area. I've been through it. I didn't grow up in a mechanic's shop. My father was mechanically adept, maybe even knew a lot about car engines and tools, but being a typical kid (you know, the kind I insulted a few paragraphs back), I rejected his every effort and offer to teach me what he knew.

In fact, I grew to hate engines and mechanics. As far as I could tell, they came straight from hell. Engines and mechanics ate up any money I managed to earn. They intruded into my life at the worst possible times. The engines made hideous noises and did what they could to complicate my life. At which point, I dragged the stricken vehicle to a mechanic. Mechanics looked at me like I was an idiot, stuck the spark plug wires back on the plugs, and charged me $20 for the favor. Mechanics, I reasoned, are dirty and smell bad. They speak a language I can't understand. Clearly, mechanical things and mechanical people were to be avoided in all cases. Nothing good can be expected from mechanics and their tools and their devices, not to mention the devious, devilish machines they work on.

I nursed that resentment well into my senior years. I got to be over 50 years old without ever changing the oil in a car. My complete tool inventory was two screwdrivers—a Phillips and a slotted—and a loose, failing pair of pliers. As far as I was concerned, opening a car hood was for all the world equivalent to Pandora opening her mythical box: releasing upon mankind (or at least upon me) all the woes of the world.

I had been given a tractor 10 years earlier, a 1936 Allis-Chalmers WC. After all, a friend reasoned, if I was going to have a "farm," shouldn't I also have a tractor? So he gave me this one. From the first moments I had with her, I had profound respect for that orange tractor. It sat for years in a woodlot, covered with fallen branches, dirt, mouse and bird droppings, without any attention or care. Yet, when we poured a cup of gas in her and popped the clutch as we rolled her from her grave in those trees, she started. For the first time in my life I drove a tractor . . . up onto the trailer that brought her to my farm. You have to have respect for that kind of endurance.

Perhaps you can tell from my words here the affection I came to have for that machine. She came to be known as "Sweet Allis," here on Primrose Farm. There were lots of surprises over the years. After sitting for months in subzero temperatures, when nothing else would start, Sweet Allis did. When nothing could make it through the mud or snow, heat or cold, Sweet Allis did. And yet for another 10 years I left her care and tending to the mechanic in town, even down to something as basic as changing her oil.

Then one day, for some reason that utterly escapes me now, I decided to change her oil. And of course the oil pan plug was stuck. I went to town and asked my usual mechanic there what I could do to break loose that plug. He gave me a nearly empty bottle of penetrating oil, told me to squirt some on the plug, to lightly tap it a bit, to turn it a touch *in* before next trying to turn it out. I did all those things, and for the first time in my 50 years of life felt the utter joy of one of those little victories that make mechanicking such a pleasure. I got the plug out, drained the oil, and I slept well that night.

Not long after that, again for no reason other than divine inspiration, I thought about taking a look inside the brake box of that tractor to see if I could fix a loose brake that had plagued me for almost a decade. I turned out the two bolts that hold the cap on the brake compartment. That is without question one of the reasons people are so easily lured—make that seduced—into working with old tractors: You can look all day at an electronic or electrical device, be it a computer or a window fan, and not for the life of you be able to figure out what makes the thing run. But with an old tractor, it's all so obvious, one part connected to another. You wiggle one, and you can see right there in front of you what it then causes the other parts to do. It's like figuring out how a teeter-totter works: no genius needed there.

So I could see where the brake was. And it was obvious that these two bolts held the cap on. I cleared away the spider webs and bugs inside the casting. Hmmm. There's the brake shoe. And when you pull this lever, it tightens the shoe on that drum. Nothing complicated here. I mean, man, there it all is, just plain as can be. I'm betting if you turn this little screw here, it should tighten up that shoe. And maybe . . . yep! That's it! I did it! I fixed the brake! After all these years of total mechanical illiteracy, I actually managed to take something mechanical that didn't work and make it work! I did it! Hey, Linda, look at this—*I'm a mechanic!!!*

That did it—I was hooked. My life has not been the same since that moment. I have accumulated a collection of maybe 35 more Allis WCs, some in pretty good shape, some little more than wreckage. I now have a well-equipped shop. I've rebuilt dozens of engines and transmissions. Oh, I still don't consider myself a real mechanic. I'm still a beginner. My real job is writing. Mechanicking is my pleasure, my joy, and my therapy.

Over the years I have accumulated a lot of information and experience, however. I have talked to a lot of mechanics, tractor collectors, and restorers, as well as other writers. I have been in a lot of shops and read a lot of books. Oh, I'm an expert at what it's like to be a beginner, but I'm not an expert mechanic. That's what qualifies me to write this book for you: I've not only been there, I'm *still* there. Like a Zen mechanic, what's important is not that I know the answers but that I know the questions!

Right off, I want to make sure you understand that this is not a book that is going to make you an expert. In anything. It is not an encyclopedia, or manual, or even an introduction to tractor restoration, repair, or mechanicking. Nope, I just want to help you out with some terminology and guidance so the next time you try to have a conversation about old tractors with a gearhead friend, spouse, buddy up at the tavern, child or grandchild, you won't sound like a complete idiot. Like I did for years. This is not a book for people who want to become tractor nuts or who are tractor nuts, but for folks who have to put up with tractor nuts.

I live in a small town of 352 souls, and if you're in any way connected with old tractors or someone else who is connected with old tractors, you may be in a small community too. If your little town is anything like mine, everyone knows everyone else. While it may be convenient in cities to address each other as Mr. Smith or Ms. Jones, in a small town there just isn't enough time for such niceties, so we are on a first-name basis.

Sort of, but not exactly. The fact of the matter is, most folks around here operate on a *nickname* basis. It's not "Bob," "Dan," and "Dennis." It's "Bagger," "Slack Time," and "Bondo." And as with the examples I have cited here, a good two-thirds of the nicknames arise from something really dumb the guy said or did.

My hope is that this book will save *you* the indignity of being known the rest of your life as "Monkey Wrench," "Lug Nut," or "PTO," because you were once in the middle of a conversation with a bunch of tractor nuts, tried to say something intelligent, and blurted out the dumbest thing they'd ever heard. Or maybe "Muffler Grease," "Spring Water," or "Bumper Bolt," because you fell for one—or more—of the dumbest shop gags in the world, being sent to fetch a nonexistent tool or part so everyone can point and laugh at the idiot who went to the NAPA store to pick up a box of 100 rpm's for a stalling engine. I won't be able to rescue you from every potential shop or tractor peril, but hopefully I can save you from some of the worst.

As every author knows all too well, there are crowds of people out there who read things like this book with one intention in mind: to pounce on the idiot who wrote it and point out omissions and errors, no matter how insignificant, no matter how goofy. Well, let me save you some trouble and ink here: Since this book is in no way intended to be comprehensive, it is *not* comprehensive. Of course there are omissions! I not only had to draw the line somewhere, I had to draw it in thousands of somewheres—what to include, what not to include. What does a newcomer to old tractors need to know? What can I skip before turning this into a hopelessly intimidating encyclopedia? Not to mention that I am something of a beginner myself, which is why I am writing this book, so I have omitted some things because I don't know about them!

Moreover, you don't start someone down the path of learning how to read by tossing the complete collection of William Shakespeare's works in front of them. Hey, that is a paragon of the English language, right, so why not? Because first steps are first steps, that's why. I not only don't know how a magneto works, I wouldn't include that kind of information in here even if I did because this is an *introduction*, a beginning, the first step.

If you are an expert, or just a veteran or a specialist, and you are unhappy with what I am telling newcomers in these pages, let me suggest a more practical step than scolding me: take a newcomer or two aside and set them straight. Invite them into your shop and introduce them to the wonders of the International F-14, or the magneto, or a Cub's gearing system. Don't argue with *this* preacher; start your own congregation!

Now, I've published three dozen or so books before this one, so I know that there are still some of you out there just itching to find something wrong in these pages that you can point to with evident glee to show that you are smarter than I am and you should have written the book. And it won't do me any good to spit back at you that, then what the heck, why *didn't* you write the book, smarty-pants? So, here's what I've done: I have purposely put four errors in the information in this book. Four obvious mistakes. Now, see if you can find them. If you don't get these four—all four—then *you* are the idiot, and MBI made a wise decision in picking the guy who was not the dumbest rock in the box to write it.

If you are a newcomer and get really serious about this old tractor stuff, so much so that you are actually considering getting into the hobby yourself, then after you read this book, you need to get as serious about your information as you will with your tools and machinery. That is, it'll be time to specialize. And don't tell me you have no intentions of getting into actually working with old tractors. I know the words because I've said them myself: "You must be nuts! I'm not about to bust my knuckles, burn my clothes, stink like rotten gas, burn all the hair off my arms, drop a jack on my toes, or pour dirty oil in my shoes. That's for gearheads, and I'm no *gearhead*! You wouldn't catch me dead with a wrench in my hands. What a waste of money and time! Not me. Not a chance. Dumbest thing I can imagine. . . ."

No old tractor enthusiast argues with statements like that. We just nod and smile. It's like saying you've never had the flu or that you'll never fall in love. You won't even see it coming. Someone will ask if you would be interested in your grandfather's tractor, or if you need a tractor to plow the snow off the lane of your acreage, then why not get a machine that will be worth more every day you own it rather than less? Suddenly, there you'll be, all googly-eyed, in love with a big old hunk of rusting iron, buying tools and parts, asking old guys in town what the heck a PTO is, asking if anyone knows how to adjust the valves on a Ford N. At that point, you are beyond this book and you need to become an enrolled student rather than a weekend visitor to the Campus of Tractor University.

Or maybe a graduate student. Think about it: A medical doctor spends a lot of years learning his business and yet he or she only has two models of machine to work with, number 1 male and your basic number 2 female. That's it. But a tractor mechanic has to consider dozens—many dozens—of makes: Ford, Allis, Deere, Minneapolis-Moline, Oliver, International, Huber, Cockshutt. And what's worse, even within one make like Allis, there are many models—WCs, WDs, CAs, Gs, Us—and even within a certain model there are variations from year to year and tractor to tractor.

That's why I can't be comprehensive in these few pages, nor do I need to be. Once you get to the point where you need to know more about a specific tractor, then you turn to the experts. You read books, manuals, parts guides, and magazines dealing with specific makes or specific parts of specific makes. It's hard to explain this part of the passion to an outsider but I was once reading in bed, deep into a book, when Linda turned to me and said, "Rog, what are you reading?" I showed her the diagram of an Allis WC belt pulley I was studying. She sighed and said, "It used to be that when you were breathing that hard, I knew you were looking at a girlie magazine."

No kidding, it's like that. There are lots of sources of that kind of reading (tractor books, not girlie magazines). I strongly recommend the parts lists, guides, and manuals for specific tractors to be found in the catalog of Jensales (PO Box 277, Clarks Grove, MN 56016, 1-800-443-0625, www.jensales.com). For books about tractors, restoration, and genuine mechanicking, take a look at the extensive catalog of the publisher of this book, MBI Publishing, Suite 200, Galtier Plaza, 380 Jackson Street, St. Paul, MN 55101-3885, 1-800-458-0454, www.motorbooks.com. If you would like reassurance that you're not the only idiot who has made the kind of mistake you just made while working in your shop on a tractor—or are just about to make—then you need to read another of my several other tractor books, again available from MBI.

I cannot stress this point enough: the moment—the *moment!*—you have an idea of which specific make and model of tractor you are interested in, buy the parts book and operator's manual for that tractor! (Again, Jensales is the best source I have found for these publications.) If you acquire a tractor, or if your spouse or friend acquires a tractor and you want to stay in the conversations, you want to get your hands on the manual and parts book for that tractor.

In fact, I would suggest that if you are only interested in old tractors, or in lots of old tractors, that you buy one set of manuals and parts books for one particular tractor just to study so that you get a general idea of how tractors work. The detail in these operator's manuals, books, and repair manuals is amazing. They have exploded diagrams showing each and every part, pin, and nut on a tractor; descriptions of how things go together and work; details on the variations from model to model; lists of parts *and their manufacturer's numbers* so you can order new parts if they are available; maintenance procedures, on and on. In fact, I would go so far as to say that it would be foolish, if not impossible, to have a relationship with a tractor, even if it's simply a matter of having a good friend who has one, without owning a set of the manuals for that tractor.

For specific problems you encounter as you actually work on a tractor (as opposed to standing around the shop watching someone else make the mistakes), I have a couple of pieces of advice for you: First, talk with a genuine mechanic in a small town, not necessarily the guy who is making a living as a mechanic because his time is valuable, but the guy who has a reputation for knowing a lot about your kind of machine and who mostly putters and so has time to chat. Second, go to a website specializing in your kind of tractor. I am especially fond of Yesterday's Tractors Co. (www.ytmag.com), Ageless Iron (talk.agriculture.com), and the Antique Tractor Internet Service (www.atis.net) sites. As so often is the case today, these public forums are sometimes beset by the unsolicited opinions of radical religious and political throwbacks who were apparently never taught any manners by their mothers and so treat everyone who is not as nutty as they are like traitors and/or heretics. Parents should exercise caution when sending young tractor enthusiasts to tractor chat pages, which is unfortunately true for just about any website. It's a shame that idiots abuse freedom. Even many adults who use these informational tractor sites subscribe, go online, and post their questions, and then unsubscribe a couple days later after they have gotten the information or help they need, just to avoid the ugliness that pops up among the really helpful postings.

Wherever you go, you will find some helpful souls who are especially generous with newcomers to the field. You'll be amazed at the quality and quantity of expertise you can get from all over the world about the most unlikely problems imaginable. If you spend much time at a site like Yesterday's Tractors, you will find that you are soon a member of a community of friends, talking about all sorts of things from the weather to personal relationships, and sometimes even tractors. There are some posters who, although informed and helpful about tractor questions, can be overbearing and intimidating: ignore them. Believe me, what they know about tractors is often more than compensated for by what they don't now about everything else!

Who exactly is a "mechanic?" Well, that's a relative term. When it comes to working with old tractors, it sure doesn't have anything to do with certificates and diplomas hanging on the wall. Actually, the best mechanics when it comes to old tractors are folks who've learned the hard way: from experience. That's one of the things I love about it all. If you intend to learn about old tractors, you're not going to be attending boring classes; you won't be listening to some snooty professor with fancy language but not much real-life experience; there will be no theorist with lots of book learning but no common sense. Nope, the real professors when it comes to old tractors are men and women who have a lot of black dirt and grease under their fingernails. Your classrooms are going to be other shops and conversations at the Co-op or tavern. No textbooks either, although now and again you'll find yourself poring over owner's manuals or tech guides, or maybe even drooling over a tool catalog.

Sometimes your mechanic guru may have a well-equipped shop with gleaming walls and drawers of Snap-on tools that might just as well be made of gold for what they cost. But some of the best mechanics I've encountered had one greasy, old wooden box with a broken and rewelded Crescent wrench in it, a couple of bent screwdrivers, a length of baling wire, and a world of knowledge, all in a dirt-floored, converted garage with a single naked light bulb hanging from the ceiling by its wire. Choose your instructors well, but don't judge by appearances. While it's always an advantage to find an old-timer who has experience with tractors, especially the kind of tractor you are going to work with, even a competent lawn-mower mechanic is a good start.

Who is the *new* mechanic? That's not only a difficult question, it's almost an impossible one. In fact, it's one of the great surprises of America's new fascination with old tractors. The new mechanic is, well, *you*! And just as you might be anyone, the next tractor enthusiast you meet could be anyone. When I wrote my first book on old tractors, the title was *Old Tractors and the Men Who Love Them*. Man, was that ever a mistake! I quickly learned that it isn't just men who love tractors, and as you have perhaps noticed, I'm a little more cautious in my use of male pronouns when I talk about those who twist bolts and bang on stuck cylinders. Yes, most tractor enthusiasts I've met are old-timers, or at least mature men, but just as you should be prepared to find women working on a balky transmission, there are kids out there too.

You might think an old *tractor* restorer would be a farmer or someone who has a history with agriculture. Nope, can't count on that either. In fact, I would say right offhand that in my experience, farmers constitute a minority of the tractor nuts. My computer programmer is a tractor guy. And my doctor. The husband of the teller where we do our banking? Tractor guy. My father-in-law is a retired Goodyear factory worker, and an enthusiast for John Deere B tractors. You can't expect to scratch a tractor collector, restorer, or looney tune and expect to find, well, anything in particular. Once you start asking around about tractors, you're going to be amazed at who pops up with the answers.

You can't be too specific. Above I said something, for example, about *America's* fascination with old tractors. Think again, Rog. This interest is world-wide. It's astonishing. There are tractor restorers in Denmark, South Africa, and New Zealand just as surely as in Nebraska, California, and North Carolina. I have yet to meet him—or her—but there's not a doubt in my mind that some-where in the bowels of Manhattan (New York, not Kansas!) someone has an old tractor tucked away where it can be seen, appreciated, and loved.

I'm always reluctant to think of myself, much less call myself, a "mechanic." That word carries a certain air of expertise, professionalism, and, okay, *income* about it. I once told a good friend of mine that I was headed back to my place to spend the day in my shop working on a tractor. "You're not going to . . . you're not going to . . . to . . . to . . . *tinker?*" he sputtered. And I had to admit that I was going to go down there to my shop to tinker. I don't know enough to be a mechanic. It's not that serious of a thing for me. Oh, I love my tractors, my days in the shop, my tools, my shop, my tractor friends, but in all honesty, my time with these things is more along the line of fun, more a hobby or therapy than honest mechanicking. Call yourself what you will, my friend, but I recommend some caution before you assume the mantle of "mechanic." I have no trouble with tinkerer, so call me a tinkerer.

Good grief, we can't even answer with any certainty the question: What is an old tractor? Not as easy a question to answer as you might expect. Frankly, I don't think it matters why you're in the shop. Or what you're working on. Hog oilers, windmill motors, vacuum cleaners, all the same to me. But I've chosen tractors. Allis-Chalmers WCs, to be specific. Again, doesn't matter. John Deeres, Minneapolis-Molines, Hubers, Olivers, doesn't matter. A little bit of everything, one specific make and model, no big deal. One tractor in your entire life, or a constant string of wrecks, one after the other: It's all mechanicking. In my case, it's all tractor mechanicking.

There are no prizes for working on really *old* tractors, or relatively new ones. Or big or little ones. While I suppose most people think of agricultural tractors when the topic comes up, one of my best friends is working on a Huber road grader at the moment. And "tractor?" I guess the word in its most specific sense means an agricultural machine meant for farm work—for pulling implements for various crops, for moving farm equipment, for sawing wood or grinding chicken feed, planting or picking crops—in short, for working. Fundamentally, however, a tractor is a tool, a mobile mechanic device for delivering power and helping human beings accomplish a task, carry out work, speed tasks, and move things.

Not that most hobbyists like me think of their prizes as working machines. Some people like to pull weights or weighted sleds to see who has done the best job of rebuilding, souping up, or tuning their equipment. I use some of my tractors for plowing snow, grading roads, planting, or watering trees. For most of us, our tractors are objects of love and pleasure. We like to show off our handy work, drive them in parades, take kids on rides, or in my case, simply drive to town for the mail. I enjoy an open-air ride, with the sound and smell of a good ol' tractor, waving to friends and neighbors who sometimes let me know that they take pleasure in seeing ol' Rog on ol' Sweet Allis, still popping along—both of them.

You will be surprised at the variety of devices you will find included in the "tractor" category. There are huge ones and small ones. One of my favorites is my Allis G, more of a garden tractor or motorcycle than what you think of as a *tractor*. Fitting quite nicely within the category "tractor," there are the Gravely and David Bradley machines that are little more than glorified rototillers on one end, then on up the size scale to monsters like the Oliver OC-18 crawler at 35,000 pounds! That's quite a range when you think about it, and there is someone somewhere who is working on one of these tractors, whatever size, and loving it as if it were a good dog, good friend, or a favorite tool.

The idea of a "tractor" is actually quite recent, if you think about it: less than 100 years old. After all, the internal combustion engine is not exactly archeological. The systematic, presumed use of tractors in farming is included in only about half of those years. I'm 69 years old, but I remember quite well being at my Uncle Fred and Aunt Mary's farm when horses were a part of their haying operation. My cousin Dick and I were always riding the workhorses around his place and so was every other kid in the area. Workhorses were as standard a piece of equipment as a tractor. The tractor I most admire—the Allis-Chalmers WC—was manufactured as late as 1948 (and as early as 1933), which makes most of my "antique" tractors younger than me! My beloved Sweet Allis rolled off the assembly line in West Allis, Wisconsin, the same year I was carried out of a Lincoln, Nebraska, hospital: 1936. In fact, it was almost exactly the same month. The biggest difference is that Sweet Allis still starts every morning and I don't.

You are going to find people admiring "old" tractors that were manufactured in the 1960s, maybe even the 1970s. There may be some discussion in old-tractor circles about what constitutes "old" or "antique," but I've never seen or heard them. Nor do I want to—I think that's a silly concern. They're tractors. And they're older than computers. That's enough for me, and apparently it's enough for most folks who love tinkering with rusty machinery, so that should be good enough for you too.

One gets the impression that while automobiles seem to have been working toward some standardization, tractors were still a subject of a lot of experimentation until very recently, and maybe they still are today. To me, all cars look alike. However, the differences in old tractors will boggle even the most adaptable mind. That means that while I try to describe and define various aspects of old tractors to you, as well as outline their function and use, you are going to have to keep in mind that the part I am describing—say, a water pump—may look different on the tractor you are looking at, it may be in a different location than I suggest, or it may not be there at all. (Each of my Allises has a water pump on the front of the engine, right behind the radiator and the fan blade, but Linda's John Deere B doesn't have a water pump at all!) For this kind of detailed information, you need to turn to those specific books, magazines, websites, and human resources I've mentioned above.

Admittedly, our task here is going to be a little simpler than it might be with an automobile, because we are working with tractors, which are essentially tools: stripped down, strictly utilitarian, no-nonsense tools. As you will quickly find, tractors don't allow for a lot of accommodation for human operators. In fact, it may take you some time to figure out how to climb up on the darned thing, and then where to put your feet and hands. While tractor engines and transmissions are paragons of engineering genius, you'll wonder who the idiot was who thought you could operate a handbrake, hand throttle, hand clutch, gear shift, and steering wheel all at the same time, with only two hands.

In fact, I get the impression that old tractors were designed and built more with the mechanic in mind than the operator. That's certainly one of the things I enjoy about my Allis WCs—they are easy to get to, easy to work on, easy to understand. As you will figure out, I'm an *old*-tractor guy in part because I don't know much—and don't really *want* to know much—about hydraulics and electrical systems. My WCs don't have hydraulic systems, and there is a sum total of four wires on the engine: a length of wire to each of the four spark plugs. That's it. Four wires. And a magneto, which no one understands, so I don't worry about that very much.

I was once told that the Allis WC engine was designed so that you could lift out the engine and set it across the side rails, making it possible to rebuild the engine right out in the field, which was probably a good thing because precious few farmers had actual shops or could afford a professional mechanic with a shop. The phrase "shade-tree mechanic" was not a fancy metaphor; most mechanics then and a few even now threw a stout chain over a large tree branch and hauled the engine out of the tractor to rebuild it out in the rain and sun.

That's another attraction of old tractors: You don't need a lot of fancy tools to work on them. It is the rare old tractor on which you will find a Phillips screw; in fact, the Phillips screwdriver wasn't even invented until the mid-1930s (Yep, by a guy named Phillips!). There are no metric nuts, no computer terminals, no fasteners with sockets in the head for tools with little stars, squares, or triangles. There's a lot of room for mistakes on old tractors, and tinkerers like me tend to make mistakes. The tolerances are gigantic and you wind up using your fingernail more often than a micrometer. I use a torque wrench to be sure nuts and lugs are close to factory specs, but how many farmers do you think had torque wrenches handy when they were rebuilding a tractor engine out in the field in 1935?

A real advantage of working on old tractors for fat, old guys like me is that you can work on them standing up! Or you can at least be lying comfortably on your back with plenty of room for your elbows and knees.

When it comes to the world of old tractor enthusiasts, perhaps the biggest question without a real answer is: "What is it with old tractors anyway?" Believe me, skeptics and onlookers ask that question out loud a million times a day all around the world. I don't know what the big deal with old tractors is, to tell you the truth, or why so many of us get so goofy about them. Some folks work on an old tractor that has a family history; it belonged to Grandpa, or Dad, or an uncle. Or it's the model that Grandpa had. Maybe it's a rare tractor that just happened to fall into your hands, or maybe it's the most common tractor in your area. In my case, a friend gave me my first Allis WC. I came close to buying a John Deere B at the time, and if I had, I'm sure I would have wound up being a Greenie instead of an Orangie.

For some, the attraction to old tractors is the attraction to the past and to history. For others, it may be an affection and respect for agriculture. I think we all have a kind of primal appreciation for farming. We all seem to have at least one farm in our past and it is drenched with the gravy of nostalgia. For me, it's my Uncle Fred and Aunt Mary's farm in Eastern Wyoming. I don't suppose I spent a lot of days there, but the time I did spend is etched in my mind forever. Maybe that's part of what old tractors mean to me. I can't say for sure.

Frankly, I don't think it matters what you are collecting, restoring, or repairing, or why you are doing it. You shouldn't have to explain it to anyone, and certainly not apologize for it. The main thing is that you have plenty of compatriots in this wacky pursuit. Sure, you'll hear all kinds of kidding about what color of tractor is best, or what model. Maybe you'll even hear some serious arguing about that silly issue. The bottom line is that there is a brotherhood and sisterhood of old iron that shares a lot more than divides it. Once tractor nuts get past the preliminaries of what color their tractors are, you will find that underneath the paint there is a profound affection we all share for old machinery, old iron, or ways and technologies and ideas. That's where the fun is.

To be a part of that fun, it helps to know the language, and that is the purpose of this book. It would be impossible to give you every term you need, so I am going to deal with only the most common and most basic. To find out all the other more exotic terms—ridge reamers, throw-out bearings, wet clutch vs. dry clutch, stubby wrenches, offset wrenches, Stillson wrenches, left-handed metric pipe wrenches, that kind of thing—you need to spend some time in a shop with a real mechanic, read manuals and guides to the specific tractor you have sitting there in front of you, ask around, visit some tractor shows, and hang around some tavern tables when the talk is about old tractors. Then you're in for the real fun.

Old-Tractor Rule Number One: This is a hobby where time has no relevance. If that tractor of yours has been sitting in a woodlot for 40 years waiting for you, accumulating a patina of bird poop and rust, there's obviously no hurry in getting it back into working condition. *Take your time and do it right* seems to be this hobby's prime directive. As lonely as the hours in your shop might be, there is a strong society of friends and old masters who are eager to share with you what they know, and maybe even some spare parts they have stacked out in the back of their shop. And maybe that's another rule of the hobby: It's more about learning than knowing. The excitement is about entering and exploring a new world, an exotic technology, a system totally apart from all the day-to-day, boring, dreary things we do to make a living. There is a lot to be learned, after all—welding, machining, paint techniques, terminology, techniques, safety procedures, and maybe even a few traditional stories and jokes. (Not the least of what you'll find in these pages are the kinds of things you need to know *not* to go out to find when the old-time mechanic sends you: for example, muffler bearing grease, or maybe a gallon of spring water for the radiator, because it never freezes, you know.)

I apologize for omissions and errors you might find (or not find) here, but just as when I'm out in my shop banging away on some old iron, I'm doing my best. (And there *are* those four mistakes I put in here on purpose, don't forget!) Now, pull up that old stool over there and sit down. We're ready to get you started on what you need to know to talk about old tractors with old-timers without sounding like a dang fool.

There are a lot of terms to explain here, and I can't explain or define some of them without using some of the others, so in some cases I'll be talking about one piece of a tractor while using words and terms I haven't explained yet. Just be patient. Sooner or later, I'll get to everything. If you feel you can't understand item number one unless you get some idea of what item number two is, check the index at the rear of the book and take a quick glance at item number two in advance. Or thumb through the book until you find it. To make this easier, as I deal with each item, I will capitalize in bold the entire word the first time it appears in the section devoted to it to make it easier for you to find. I hope this isn't too confusing. It's going to be tough enough, after all, to dismantle a tractor and explain all the parts to you! If you know much about tools, machinery, tractors, that kind of thing, you will probably think that sometimes I am being way too simplistic, even patronizing. Well, I figure it's better to make things a bit too basic or simple than to make them a bit too complicated. The book is meant, after all, for beginners.

CHAPTER 1

ENGINE

Already we have a problem with our nomenclature: that big, hot, iron thing that makes automobiles go—you know, that thing under the hood with all the wires, pipes, and tubes sticking out of it? The thing that makes all the noise? That's the ENGINE. Well, at least in an automobile it's an engine. In a tractor, for no particular reason I can figure out, it's called a MOTOR. That makes no sense at all. Everywhere else, a motor is an electrical drive mechanism. In a tractor, the engine is the motor. All I can do about that dictionary confusion is offer my apologies. However, this distinction is a coded password into the world of old tractor nuts; if you call that tractor engine the *motor* in your next discussion with some old tractor nut, you're already going to look like you know a lot more than you actually do.

The BLOCK is pretty much the main part of the engine, otherwise known as the "motor." (Some folks from here in town were once on a trip through the barren Nebraska Sandhills—still essentially on the frontier—and stopped at a small town tavern. The ladies started ordering things like "fuzzy navels," "strawberry daiquiris," and other frilly froufrous that usually come with little paper umbrellas in fancier drinkeries. Finally, the grizzled bartender put down his order pad and said, "Uh, look here, let's make this simple: How many whiskies, how many beers?" Let's agree to do the same thing from now on in these pages: motor, engine, it's all the same, okay?)

Now, where was I? Oh yeah, the block. It's that big "block" of iron in the front part of the tractor (now and then—but rarely—it's in the rear part, like with an Allis model G) that provides the power for the vehicle. The block is made of cast iron (not steel) and it houses the cylinders and pistons that contain the little explosions of fuel that are the heart of the INTERNAL COMBUSTION engine (uh, motor!). Most accessories are hung on the block, such as the water pump, oil pump, magneto or generator, filters, radiator, and transmission, all of which will be discussed in their own sections below. (It is *internal* combustion—burning inside—that contrasts with the older *external* combustion *steam* engine, where the fire that provides the power is on the outside. This probably isn't the most precise technical definition for the terms, since this would make a horse an internal combustion engine, but then well, uh, you know.)

Although the motor won't work without almost every single other component that is fastened on it or in it, the very principle of internal combustion requires a place for that combustion—burning—to take place within, and that place is the block. Or more specifically, in the CYLINDERS. (Actually it takes place in the COMBUSTION CHAMBERS at the top of the cylinders, but that's getting beyond the scope of this book.) The block is not solid iron. Inside the massive block, the largest single piece of metal on the whole tractor, there is a lot of empty space. Cylinders may be bored directly into the solid metal of the block—a BORED CYLINDER—or separate metal cylinders may be fitted into a more open, less solid block—a SLEEVED BLOCK or SLEEVED CYLINDER.

If you get a chance, I strongly suggest that you drop by your local small-engine shop and ask the proprietor for an old discarded lawn-mower, chain saw, or weed whacker engine. Tell him what you're up to, and he'll probably even help you get that thing opened up. It'll be a lot easier to get into and learn about how internal combustion works from a smaller example than a full-size tractor engine . . . uh, motor. I don't think I'll ever get that straight.

To put it simply, an internal combustion engine gets its power when a small amount of fuel (usually gasoline) and air are sucked into the cylinder and ignited (usually by an electrical spark). The burning mixture of fuel and air is contained in a small space (the combustion chamber mentioned above) and has nowhere to go. At the bottom of the cylinder there is a movable blockage called a piston. The explosion forces that piston down the cylinder a few inches. A rod connects the piston to a heavy steel shaft that converts the up-down motion of the piston into a turning action, and that's the action that makes the wheels turn.

You may hear a piston referred to as OVERSIZE or a cylinder as a REBORE. When cylinders (or sleeves) are excessively or unevenly worn, they may have to be rebored; that is, the holes must be redrilled. In that case, of course, the hole is bigger. Because the hole is bigger, the pistons have to be bigger, or at least the rings must be just a touch bigger to ensure a tight fit between the piston and the cylinder. The pistons and rings are then oversize, and the cylinder is a rebore.

Since the word TOLERANCE is used through the mechanics of a tractor, in almost every component, maybe this would be a good place to give a brief explanation of it. Obviously machine parts are meant to fit firmly, even tightly, but there does need to be a certain amount of looseness or tolerance built in. This is a word I love when it comes to old tractors, ah, tolerance! Good in human relations, even better in tractor mechanicking!

When you hear gearheads—a term I use and accept with glowing enthusiasm and pride, by the way—talking about stroke and bore, they are referring to the distance a piston travels on each of its trips up and down in the cylinder (STROKE) and the diameter of the cylinder in which it moves (BORE). Moreover, references to cubic inches or cubic centimeters (CCs) allude to the amount of volume in that stroke and bore.

Antique tractors permit astonishing tolerances, or, in my case, sloppiness and error. If you mis-torque a bolt, misjudge a shim, or forget a spacer, they just go ahead and run anyway. I advise doing the very best you can when you are working on machinery. Get things done as carefully and accurately as you possibly can. That only makes sense. But do know that old iron will work with you on these things, no matter how inept or green you are. That's important to guys like me.

Inside the block there are anywhere from 1 to 12 cylinders. It is within these tubes where the fuel and air are mixed and detonated, causing the millions of combustions that give the tractor the power to move and drive all sorts of other equipment. Most tractors have 2 or 4 cylinders, but there is plenty of variation including 3-cylinder Porsches. (Porsche *tractors*, that is.) Sometimes the cylinders are bored or cast directly into the metal of the blocks; sometimes steel SLEEVES are inserted inside the block and serve as cylinders. There are wet and dry sleeves, depending on whether the coolant (again, to be discussed below) comes into direct contact with the sleeves or not.

The cylinders are actually open at both ends. To contain the fuel explosions, something has to be attached or inserted in the cylinder. At one end there is the HEAD, a heavy, iron cap that is bolted onto the block. The head is usually also the location of the valves that let air and fuel in and exhaust—burned gases—out of the motor. The head usually sits on top of the block, but don't count on that; sometimes cylinders are horizontal and the head is therefore on the front or rear "side" of the motor. Between the head and the block is a relatively soft metal and fiber compound sheet called the HEAD GASKET. There are a lot of gaskets on a tractor—on any piece of machinery, in fact—but this one is a biggie. It is usually the most expensive gasket on a tractor because it is the one that takes the real punishment when the engine is operating. The head gasket seals the space between the head and the block. It is exposed to the heat and pressure of the burning gases in the cylinders. There's a lot of strain there!

The head is held onto the block by threaded rods or STUDS. The term *threaded* means the rods have little grooves cut around each end so they can be turned into threaded holes in the block, or have nuts turned onto them to hold the head firmly onto the block.

So, the fuel burns within a cylinder capped by the head—what keeps the force of the explosion from just blowing out the end of the tube opposite the head (usually the bottom)? Ah ha! In that answer lies the real secret of the internal combustion engine! At the other end of the cylinder is the PISTON. The piston is a metal plug that rides smoothly and easily up and down in the cylinder. Pistons are attached by rods to a heavy metal shaft—the CRANKSHAFT (more on this below)—inside the engine. As the pistons go up and down in the block, they turn the crankshaft. The burning of the fuel is timed so that it occurs precisely at the moment the plug—that is to say, the piston—slides up to the top of the cylinder. The fuel burns and with incredible violence—you'd be amazed at what a nasty fire a very small amount of hot, vaporized, compressed gasoline can make—and drives the piston back down to the bottom of the cylinder, at the same time rotating the crankshaft. Again, I hope you can find a small engine you can dismantle and study so you can see the really beautiful motion, smoothness, and precision with which this generation and transfer of power takes place in an engine. It's a gorgeous thing to see, especially if you are a gearhead like me.

Since this is meant to be an introduction to newcomers in the Wide World of Tractoring, there's not room here for a detailed discussion of the operation of the internal combustion engine. Almost all larger engines, like tractor motors, are FOUR-CYCLE or FOUR-STROKE engines. This means that each piston makes four movements for each time fuel is burned in the cylinder to produce power. The piston goes down in the cylinder as the intake valve opens, sucking in a mixture of fuel and air in what is called the INTAKE STROKE.

Then the piston goes back up, compressing the fuel and air—the COMPRESSION STROKE. Gasoline by itself is ferociously explosive stuff—the pinch of it that is taken into that cylinder is already dangerous—but now it has been heated in the intake manifold, which makes it even more volatile, and yikes! Now it is packed tightly in the cylinder by that piston. It really doesn't matter what kind of fuel you have in there—kerosene, distillate, tractor fuel—I'm telling you, when that spark plug makes a tiny little spark just as the piston swings past the top of its path, that burning fuel charge is powerful enough to move great hulks of iron, which is exactly what that motor is supposed to be doing.

Then the piston goes back down as the fuel burns, pressing ferociously down on the piston in what is called the POWER STROKE. Finally, the piston moves back up in the cylinder as the exhaust valve opens and the burned gases are blown out the exhaust pipe.

There are also TWO-CYCLE or TWO-STROKE engines that tend to be less efficient. These engines are the kind of thing you are likely to find on smaller items such as chain saws and lawn mowers. Briefly and very simply put, the power stroke, intake stroke, exhaust, and compression stroke are all combined in a two-stroke engine.

When you hear someone use the word "STUCK" in connection with a tractor, they are usually talking about the motor. The stuck thing is usually a piston, seized up in a cylinder. Again, the vocabulary is strictly that of the tractor world: automobile engines are usually "frozen," or "seized." In the contrary world of old tractors, rather than a frozen engine, it's a stuck motor. Other parts can be stuck too: a crank- or camshaft, a valve or valve rocker arm, a transmission, or a wheel bearing. It all means the same thing: that tractor isn't going to move for a while.

This situation sounds worse than it is. I love it when I find a tractor for sale with a stuck motor. That means you can stand there shaking your head, clicking your tongue, and making motions of frustration and futility. Maybe let tears well up in your eyes as you consider the sad fate of this once noble machine, and then make an offer that sounds for all the world like you are doing this guy a favor by hauling away his pile of junk, his *stuck* pile of junk.

Frankly, I don't think a stuck engine is a big deal. I see it as a challenge and delight. It may not take much to get that motor (or transmission) free and running again, but even if you have to dismantle the motor and remove the offending piston with a sledgehammer, it's not that big of a problem in the long run. I do strongly advise that you avoid using force for as long as you possibly can. You can gently rock a tractor while it is in gear to see if you can maybe free up a stuck piston, but chaining it behind another tractor, getting it up to road speed, and then popping the clutch is a sure path to a broken rod, shattered block, and totally ruined tractor motor.

The real secret in breaking anything loose that is stuck on an old tractor, from pistons to the smallest nuts and bolts, is patience. Add to that plenty of good, commercial penetrating oil and very gentle pressure— light tapping with a small hammer or mallet—and mountains of time. Sooner or later you will first feel the slightest motion in the "stuck" part, then there will be clear visible movement, and finally you will gain full freedom. Nothing has been broken. That is victory.

Around the piston, which may be made of iron or aluminum, in grooves cut into its sides are the piston RINGS. They are usually three or four in number, each serving various purposes. One ring makes a tight seal between the piston and the cylinder walls so oil does not work its way up into the combustion chamber and so ignition products like exhaust gases, heat, and carbon won't fall back down into the oil pan. Another ring scrapes excess oil back down the cylinder walls to the pan, while making sure a thin film of oil remains. In some cases, the form of the rings is dramatically different and must be put onto a piston in correct order and with the right sides up and down.

When an engine is stuck, it is often the rings that are stuck against the walls of the cylinder. Rings are a bit fragile, so they may break when you try to take them out to clean them (a task best done with a tool called a PISTON RING EXPANDER), but they are easily replaced. In most cases it's a good idea to replace the rings anyway when an old engine is being rebuilt. A set of rings may be small but, like so many tractor parts, they can be ferociously expensive. Therefore, replacing them is something to be done with care and not taken lightly.

One of my favorite jobs at my shop table is cleaning pistons. I have no idea why I find it so pleasant. Mostly, I suppose, it's a matter of taking a really ugly piece of metal, cleaning it up, gently working the rings loose, and then cleaning and replacing them. Although I have to say I don't feel at all the same way about washing supper dishes.

Under the pistons there are the devices that connect them to the crankshaft, which transfers power to the TRANSMISSION (see Chapter 2), and convert the up and down motion of the pistons into a circular rotation. Inside the piston there is a short, heavy rod running across the piston—the WRIST PIN or PISTON PIN. Attached to it is a heavy connector reaching into the oil pan and to the crankshaft—the PISTON ROD. When you hear about an engine in a car race "blowing an engine" or "throwing a rod," this is the thing that breaks loose from the crankshaft or piston and goes through the side of the block. Yeah, that's something of a mechanical disaster, just as it sounds and looks. You don't want to be anywhere nearby when it happens.

When you OVERHAUL an engine, you dismantle it, check all of these parts for wear or damage, and then replace or repair them. Essentially, you rebuild the entire thing. Do not confuse the rural term for loose outer clothing with this process. "That dummy city boy is wearing his overhauls with both buttons on his side flaps done up!" is quite a different thing from "That dumb city boy bought hisself a tractor that needs a complete overhaul!" A term that may show up when someone is completely rebuilding a tractor motor is HOT TANKING. Once a motor is dismantled, one way to clean out a block completely (you can't believe how hard it is to get into all those holes, cracks, galleries, slots, grooves, channels, and crannies) is to dip the entire block for a few hours into a hot brew with a lye base. It comes out clean. Fewer and fewer commercial shops do hot tanking because of the problems involved to dispose of the lye, but there are still some small, amateur shops and mechanics who do it on their own. I had a friend here in my little town in the middle of nowhere who had a setup with a derrick, block and tackle, and 60-gallon drum. He does hot tanking for his own work and that of friends. We all need friends like that.

The CRANKSHAFT is the very heavy, rotating steel shaft that runs through the engine to which the bottoms of the piston rods are attached. These are attached loosely so that the shaft still turns easily, but they are firm enough that there is no slack left to allow the rods to be slammed with ferocious force against the shaft. The crankshaft rotates in the block through MAIN BEARINGS, which are sheets of alloy that allow the shaft to turn smoothly, often direct oil to it, and allow wear without requiring replacement of the entire block when things get too loose in there. It's still a job to replace main or rod bearings, requiring pretty much the removal and dismantling of the entire engine, but it is still cheaper and easier than replacing the entire block.

Along the length of a crankshaft are shiny parts that revolve within the main bearings. Those are the MAIN BEARING JOURNALS. Other parts revolve around the ends of the rod's swivel: the CONNECTING ROD JOURNALS.

The crankshaft turns inside the bottom of the rod, where it is held by a ROD CAP, a semicircular piece that continues the circle made by the bottom of the rod around the shaft. It is bolted onto the rod. Inside the circle formed by the rod and the rod cap are thin strips of metal usually made of an alloy called "babbitt," a soft mixture of antimony, tin, and copper named after Isaac Babbitt, an American inventor from the nineteenth century. (I knew you were wondering about that.) These strips, called CONNECTING ROD BEARINGS, form a protective layer between the rod and cap and the crankshaft. They can be replaced a whole lot cheaper than the rod or cap when there is substantial wear. The same is true with the babbitt bearing liners in the main bearings. The bottoms of the rods, along with the crankshaft, are often designed to splash violently into the contents of the oil pan, thus lubricating all the moving parts in the engine below the cylinders. I'd hate to be in there when that thing is running!

There's another smaller shaft rotating in the block too. While the crankshaft is very heavy and irregular in its shape, the CAMSHAFT is smaller and straighter, and rather than having elbows and bends, the camshaft has rounded lumps along its length called CAMS. By means of the TIMING GEAR that is probably in a housing outside the block and in the front of your tractor's motor, the camshaft is geared to turn. Those lumps called cams lift a series of rods (PUSHRODS, see below) that operate the valves, which are usually installed in the head.

Okay, let's follow that action from the camshaft to the valves, usually referred to as the VALVETRAIN. As they rotate, the uneven cams along the camshaft press in precise order and time on little cups called TAPPETS. The tappets have cups in which LIFTERS or PUSHRODS fit.

One end of the lifters sits in the tappets, and the other end pushes against one end of a teeter-totter sort of arrangement called a ROCKER ARM. When the lifter pushes the back side of a rocker arm up, the other side goes down and pushes on a VALVE STEM. The valve stem is connected to either an INTAKE VALVE or an EXHAUST VALVE. (Don't confuse the two. They are of different composition, shape, and size, and they shouldn't be mixed up when assembling a motor!) The valves then open into the cylinder, allowing fuel and air to come in or the burned exhaust gases to exit. There are usually two valves for each cylinder, one intake and one exhaust. The valves may be in the head (VALVE-IN-HEAD ENGINE) or in the block (L-HEAD ENGINE or FLATHEAD ENGINE). The valves in a flathead engine are accessible through a panel on the side of the block.

As you can imagine, the valves, exposed as they are to constant rapid movement and extreme heat, take a real pounding. In fact, valves in a tractor are exposed to temperatures in excess of 3,500 degrees Fahrenheit, go up and down hundreds of thousands of times an hour, travel more than a quarter-mile for every mile the vehicle travels, and take sledge-hammer blows of over a quarter-ton every time the spark plug in that cylinder fires!

Which also means that they get a lot of wear. You are likely to hear words like "VALVE GRINDING," "SEAT DRESSING," and "LAPPING IN VALVES" around just about any shop where tractors are being worked on. If valves wear excessively where they make contact with the seat—that is, the edges of the holes in which they fit—or if they get nicked or burned at one point, they do not close tightly. That means they release compression, reducing power. The heat of escaping gases and accumulating specks of hot carbon start to burn divots, grooves, cracks, and canyons in the valve and its seat. So, the mechanic takes out the valves and regrinds the surfaces that mate with the seat. If the seat is damaged or worn, then it too may be ground down to a new, even surface. That's *dressing* the seat. After the grinding and dressing are done, a final, polishing step is lapping in the valves. This involves applying VALVE GRINDING COMPOUND, a water- or oil-based goo with very fine abrasive in it, to the valve and seat and then turning the valve back and forth on the seat to make sure it has a very close and tight fit with the seat.

The rocker arms are usually (but not always) located along a shaft called the ROCKER ARM ASSEMBLY mounted on the head inside a sheet-metal case. Along the rocker arm shaft are springs, spacers, and oilers. The stem, the part of the valves that stick out of the head or block, usually exits the head or block through a set of VALVE STEM GUIDES, one for each valve. There are lots of items to pull the valves firmly back against the VALVE SEAT, the specially hardened collar against which the opening and closing valve fits tightly to contain the compression and gases that are busily exploding and burning inside the cylinder.

Around the valve stems is a strong spring, the VALVE SPRING. These are usually held in place by KEEPERS, little wedges that hold the valve within the spring, and C-CLIPS (small pieces of metal shaped logically enough like the letter C) that slip firmly onto the valve stem to keep it from falling into the cylinder if the spring should fail or break and the keepers let that thing drop. You can imagine what would happen if a valve dropped onto that piston flailing back and forth with incredible speed and power! Or maybe you can't. I've opened up engines where just the little C-clip has fallen into the cylinder somehow (you can hardly hold onto these things because they are so small, especially if they are the wire-type of clip rather than the flat washer–type). The top of the piston has hundreds—maybe thousands—of divots where that tiny bit of metal has banged around. It's amazing. Imagine then what would happen if a much more substantial piece of the machine like a valve dropped into an operating cylinder. Yikes! There wouldn't be much left of the engine. This is a great example of the importance of a really small part in the operation of a really big thing like a tractor motor! I said above that you don't want to presume that a small part like a piston ring isn't expensive; well, you also don't want to make the mistake of thinking that a small part like a C-clip on a valve stem isn't important!

Okay, let me run through that again. The crankshaft turns and through gears it turns the camshaft. The cams on the camshaft convert its rotating motion into an up-down action that pushes up the tappets and lifters, causing the rocker arms to teeter-totter, causing the valves to open and close. Once you see it, it will make all the sense in the world to you. (If you have dismantled that lawn mower engine, you may or may not find these parts. Most tractors have four-stroke engines, while a lot of small engines are two-stroke engines and don't have valves, lifters, tappets, camshafts, and that kind of thing.)

In some tractor motor blocks there is another device tucked inside the block, extending down into the oil pan, and that's the OIL PUMP. This is a relatively simple but absolutely crucial device that takes oil from the bottom of the engine and moves it up above the block, usually redistributing it along the rocker bar assembly by gravity. Often this pump is driven by a gear built into the camshaft. From the head and rocker arm assembly, the oil trickles down through drain holes, runs down along the lifters, and tappets back into the oil pan.

Somewhere along the lines carrying the oil from the pump, the oil—or some of it, as I will explain later—often is forced through the OIL FILTER, where the worst of the contaminants—small bits of metal and carbon, and other impurities—are trapped in a disposable filter to keep the oil relatively clean. If there is a failure in the transportation of oil anywhere along the line, the result can be catastrophic for the engine. Oil not only carries away heat from the cylinders, but it also keeps everything lubricated and running smoothly. Old tractors have one of the few gauges common to them all, an OIL PRESSURE GAUGE, somewhere along the oil lines. In my WC, it's found as a part of the filter assembly. Believe me, it's something worth watching.

I've spoken about the OIL PAN several times along the way already. It is the sump container somewhere at the bottom of the motor. It's where the oil drains, collects, is splashed by the crankshaft and sucked up by the pump, and from which it is drained when it needs to be replaced with clean oil. It is usually the lowest part of the motor-engine assembly and has a plug from which the dirty oil can be drained.

There are threaded holes in the head into which the SPARK PLUGS are turned. Spark plugs provide the electrical charge to burn the gasoline-and-air mixture that drives the piston down and the makes the wheels of that tractor turn. A current of electricity is sent to the plug; a spark on the end of the plug jumps a measured gap, and that's enough to ignite the hot, compressed fuel in the cylinder. (In diesel engines there is a GLOW PLUG, which heats up the cylinder so that the fuel can be vaporized and ignited, but it is actually the heat of the high compression of the air and fuel within the diesel cylinder that ignites the mixture and provides the power. I'm not going to go into the difference between gasoline engines and diesels here, but there are differences. Most old tractors are not diesels so we won't spend any more space worrying about that issue here.)

On some tractors like the John Deere B, on the block or head not far from the spark plug, you will find a COMPRESSION RELIEF VALVE or PETCOCK. It's not easy to crank over a tractor engine. One cylinder or more is going to have both its valves closed, which means you are compressing a lot of air when you try to turn it over. It's not easy for an electrical starting motor, and it's harder still for a man with a hand crank. So some tractors—mostly one- and two-cylinder engines—ease the task by providing small valves into the cylinder that you can open to release some of the compressing air while the motor is being turned to start.

I'm not all that sure this is a good idea. Every time I start Linda's John Deere B with the compression relief valves open, raw gas is blown up my sleeve. If you can tell an Allis-Chalmers WC man by the way he holds a book he is reading off to his left, you can spot a John Deere B man because his left arm or leg always reeks of gasoline. Who thought this system up anyway? (I'll have more to say about "compression" later on.)

Once the fuel has burned, moved the piston, and powered all the other stuff attached to it in and on the motor, then the spent, hot gases are let out of the engine through the exhaust valve. The exhaust valve directs the burned fuel charge through the EXHAUST MANIFOLD, a piece of iron bolted by means of more lugs along the side or top of the engine. Look out! This thing is really hot. While the hot gases are removed from the engine through some passages in the manifold, air and fuel are sent into the engine through the INTAKE MANIFOLD by the carburetor, a word which is misspelled by almost every veteran mechanic as "carburator," for some reason. (You can save yourself a lot of trouble by using "carb" whenever you write the word down. Everyone will know what you mean.) In this incredibly hot exchange, the incoming fuel is heated to a point where it's darn near ready to burn at the slightest excuse, which is provided in your tractor motor by the spark plugs. The holes where the exhaust gas exits and the fuel enters the motor from the manifolds are called PORTS.

The outgoing exhaust gases then leave the motor, and your tractor, by traveling out the EXHAUST PIPE or STACK. The exhaust stack is not much more than a length of pipe that contains a MUFFLER, a part of the stack designed containing baffles to reduce the noise emanating from inside the cylinders. You'd be surprised—and deafened—by how loud those thousands of small fires can be without a muffler. I'm now 69 years old and mostly deaf, an affliction my doctor refers to as "Allis-Chalmers Ear." I recommend that you put mufflers on your tractors, authentic or not, and wear ear protection when working around a running engine.

About those exhaust gases: They are made up largely of a by-product of burning, *carbon monoxide*. This stuff is deadly and you want to be careful with it. Never, *never* run any engine or motor inside a closed shop. I once needed to run an engine just a short time and I figured, hey, it's just going to be a few seconds, so, why not? Okay, I thought, so carbon monoxide is lethal; I'll be careful and turn off that engine if I sense any problem at all.

Well, I did run that engine for just a few seconds in my shop, with the doors closed. I also caught myself just moments before I hit the floor. I made my way out the door and threw it open. When I was sure my head was cleared, I took a deep breath and held it and went back in to turn off that tractor. I decided to let the shop air out completely before going back in. I went to the house and told Linda how dumb I'd been—something she has never let me forget—and despite my protests, she called our doctor. He said I should be okay but that she might watch me that evening to see if I acted goofy around bedtime. "He always acts goofy around bedtime," she told him.

Don't you act that goofy, at bedtime or not. Never run an engine in a shop if the exhaust is not vented to the outside. And don't let anyone else do that either—not even a grizzled old veteran shop mechanic who insists he knows what he's doing. If he starts that engine with the doors closed, take it from me, he doesn't know what he's doing.

Outside the block, usually at the front of the motor and attached to it, right behind the radiator if there is one, is the WATER PUMP—again, if there is one, and the FAN and the FAN BELT. I'll have more to say about the cooling system later on, but since all these components are usually attached directly to the block, I figure I'll at least introduce them here. Some tractors like the John Deere B do not have water pumps. Instead, they use natural convection—hot goes up, cold goes down—to circulate coolant through the engine and radiator. If there is a water pump it is at the front of the block, often driven by a rubber fan belt that is driven by a pulley at the outside end of the crankshaft. On my Allis WCs, the water pumps are also the location for the fans that pull air back through the radiators where the heat of the motors is dissipated. After the coolant is cooled a little by the outside air, it runs back into hollows, tunnels, and passages in the block and head of the engine, often called GALLERIES.

Coolant is usually water or a combination of water and chemical coolants commonly known as antifreeze. Coolant is used for far more than keeping the water in an engine from freezing up and cracking the block or ruining the radiator. These days, modern coolants also increase the efficiency of the system in carrying off heat during the summer. They also stop leaks and lubricate seals. It's important to keep "antifreeze" in your tractor's cooling system year 'round.

Somewhere close to the tractor motor, you will find an extremely heavy iron wheel called the FLYWHEEL. If an engine just fired one cylinder after another, it would be hard to keep running because it wouldn't have any momentum to keep it spinning, driving all the timing mechanisms, activating the valves system, compressing in other cylinders, or exhausting gases. Once that heavy flywheel gets to turning, it doesn't like to stop. The flywheels on my Allis are also important because they have marks that you need to reference when TIMING the engine. Timing is setting the electrical system so the spark plugs fire at exactly the right moment in the pistons' circuits to provide the most power. The clutch is also attached to the back of the flywheel. On my Allis, the flywheel is located inside the clutch housing, and is in fact a part of the clutch mechanism, but you are liable to find a flywheel just about anywhere on an old tractor. A favorite example is the John Deere B, with the flywheel on the left side of the tractor. Not only is it outside any housing, but it is in fact accessible to the operator because it is the primary way of starting the tractor. The operator firmly grasps the flywheel, which even has little finger notches on its back side for that very purpose, and turns it to crank the engine over.

While we're at it, maybe I should say a few things about starting—and stopping—a tractor's motor. Older tractors didn't have electric starting motors (and some of us prefer our machinery like that because it makes them much simpler to operate and repair) so you started them by turning a CRANK. (Don't look up *crank* in the index of my book *Old Tractors and the Men Who Love Them*, because after the word *crank* in the index, a wiseacre editor at MBI wrote "See 'About the author . . .' ") On the John Deere B, you "crank" the engine by manually turning the flywheel; on other tractors, you started the motor by turning a hand crank, usually directly in the front of the machine. These were either permanently affixed there or inserted onto a crank spindle, used to start the motor, and then removed again.

Believe me, if you spend any time at all around old tractors and tractor people, you are soon and often going to get lessons about using a hand crank. Hand cranks are dangerous business, so pay attention to those lessons! You will also hear stories about broken arms, split lips, lost teeth, even deaths resulting from incorrect use of the hand crank, which is probably why it wasn't long before electric motors driven by storage batteries soon replaced the hand crank! Briefly, however, never turn *down* on a hand crank; pull it *up*, and only in a quarter- to half-turn. That is, don't spin that crank around in a circle! It can kick back and do ferocious damage to you. Also, when using a hand crank, be sure that your fingers and thumb are both on the same side of the handle. I know this seems pretty clumsy, but it's a lot less uncomfortable than a thumb broken and bent over backwards by a backfiring engine!

Huge engines are sometimes—even today—started with the help of a PONY ENGINE, a smaller engine that is much easier to crank and start. The pony engine's power is then used to crank and start the larger engine. Perhaps the most interesting starting system was the old Marshall tractor, which used the force of a shotgun shell to turn the engine and start it. I wonder who thought *that* one up? A friend of mine had a huge old Caterpillar tractor that was started by the operator inserting a long, heavy iron bar into a hole in the exposed flywheel and then pulling back fast and hard on the lever to turn over the engine and start it. Uh . . . thanks, but no thanks! I'm going to pass on *that* adventure.

If you are new to old tractors, you're probably wondering what needs to be said about turning a tractor *off.* You might be surprised. Why don't you just guess? Uh huh, no key. No switch. So? Not so easy, huh? On some tractors there is a kind of switch, a small metal clip on the magneto that you press to ground something or another, thus stopping the motor. I'm not an expert about magnetos; I even have my doubts whether electricity actually exists. Have you ever *seen* electricity? No, so are we supposed to take electricity on *faith?* On many antique tractors you stop the engine, uh, motor, by turning off the *fuel.* This may seem annoying—even wasteful, since it takes a while for the motor to use up the fuel already in the carburetor and lines, but this made perfect sense in earlier times. Many tractors started with gasoline but operated on a lower-grade (and usually less expensive) fuel like tractor fuel, distillate, or kerosene, so you wanted to burn off all that fuel so it wouldn't be the first thing into the cylinders the next time you wanted to start it. Or tried to start it, since you were almost certain to have problems if you didn't burn off that low-grade fuel and clear the way for the flow from the gasoline reservoir.

The various controls necessary for operating the motor (like the ignition switch, if there is one) may be found directly on the motor itself or, more conveniently, organized near where the operator is located. For example, the choke on my Allis WC is directly on the carburetor and the operator has to be standing on the ground alongside the tractor to operate it. That's okay, in order to crank the engine by hand you need to be there anyway. On my WD, on the other hand, the choke is controlled with a wire pull, again a good arrangement because the wire controlling the starter is right there beside it. I will deal with fuel controls in the chapter on liquids.

(By the way, if you want a more detailed explanation of engines and their components, I suggest that you go to the howstuffworks.com website and see the illustrations and explanations there. In fact, this a good site to look up just about any item in these pages that I haven't made clear to you.)

CHAPTER 2

TRANSMISSION

T he TRANSMISSION (also referred to as the TRANNY) is the part of the tractor that carries the power generated by the motor to the wheels that make the tractor go. On many tractors, the transmission also drives all the other turning, spinning, pumping, and rocking devices hooked up to it. Unlike most automobiles, a tractor's transmission is also expected to provide power for a number of other systems that drive a lot of other pieces of machinery like buzz saws, balers and pickers, mowers, lifts, electric generators, pumps, grinders, mills, posthole diggers, and just about everything else that might need mechanical power.

The crankshaft of the tractor's motor usually runs from the motor to a CLUTCH, which allows the rotation of the engine to be separated and thus shut off from all or some of the other things being driven by it. The clutch is, quite simply, a set of plates that can be brought together and engaged with each other by friction so that the motor supplies power to the wheels at the back end of the tractor and everything else it is powering. The lever or foot pedal that separates or joins those plates is also called the clutch. The plates in the clutch may be WET PLATES or DRY PLATES, depending on whether they run in a liquid bath or not.

Unlike automobiles where the clutch is always operated with a foot pedal or automatically with a hand lever, on old tractors there is a foot clutch, hand clutch, or both. That is in part so that a tractor can have LIVE POWER. This not a clear concept, even to veteran tractor mechanics and operators. The experts tell me that "live power" means that various drive systems other than the back wheels (but especially the PTO) continue to turn even when the power to drive the tractor's wheels is cut off by using the clutch. LIVE HYDRAULICS is a hydraulic system that continues to do its job even when the clutch is depressed, or so I'm told by those who know what they are talking about. You can imagine how convenient it is to keep equipment running even when the clutch is depressed, or conversely how *inconvenient* a tractor can be without live power and live hydraulics.

When the clutch plates are engaged—pushed together by letting out the hand lever or foot pedal—the rotation of the motor—that is, its power—is sent along the DRIVESHAFT to whatever other mechanisms that are in use: the rear-wheel drive, the buzz saw, the PTO, whatever. On my Allis WCs, which are fairly typical but not universal in their configuration, the driveshaft is connected to a BELT PULLEY sticking out the side of the frame at right angles to the driveshaft. (On my Allis C, on the other hand, the belt pulley is at the rear of the tractor, so you'll just have to look around and ask around about where the drive pulley is on the tractor you're dealing with. The belt pulley is a drum that rotates when it is engaged. A heavy canvas and rubber FLAT BELT is thrown around this drum and then around a similar drum on various pieces of equipment— usually stationary equipment like buzz saws, mills, or grinders. The pulley is engaged by a lever or (in the case of my Allis tractors) by pushing the pulley in toward the gearbox so that it engages a gear built into the driveshaft inside the tractor's transmission.

Some tractors have other outlets for power that are built in along this stage of the driveshaft, for example, the IMPLEMENT LIFT on my Allis tractors. By pressing down a pedal on the tractor with his right foot, the driver uses the mechanical power of the tractor (as opposed to hydraulic power with later model tractors) to raise and lower farming equipment like a rake or cultivator.

Somewhere along the powertrain most tractors have a PTO or POWER TAKE-OFF, one of the most useful items on a tractor. Somewhere usually at the rear of the tractor you will see a fluted (that is, SPLINED) shaft sticking out. A shaft with a female receptacle that fits firmly over this shaft can be used to carry the rotation to all manner of equipment, mobile or stationary. It is from the PTO that stationary equipment like a mill or saw can be operated without the dangers of that flapping, flailing drive belt on the drive pulley. On the other hand, believe me, the PTO, as useful as it is, is not without its dangers. In fact, it is, in my mind, the most dangerous mechanical item in all of farming. One mistake, one slip, one step too close to a revolving PTO shaft while wearing loose trousers or coat, one moment of inattention, and the operator is dead or suffers mutilation that makes him wish he were.

I'm not being funny. I once met a man who had made the horrible error of not paying attention when he stepped over a rotating PTO shaft. It caught his overalls about at his knees and pulled those parts of him near his knees, if you catch my drift, into the rapidly rotating, incredibly powerful PTO shaft. He came out of the encounter alive, but not the man he had been, either physically or mentally. I cannot stress strongly enough the danger of this part of a tractor. Power take-offs are just as dangerous on new tractors as they were on the old, and one frequently reads or hears about someone being killed or badly injured by a PTO shaft even today. On old tractors where there may be no safety shields, the danger is multiplied many times. Do whatever it takes to keep yourself and others away from a PTO shaft when it is engaged and rotating.

The PTO is engaged by pulling or pushing a lever somewhere on the tractor; this may take exploration or inquiry since there really is not a standardized form or location for the PTO control on tractors. To give you an idea how vexing this can be, on my International, the PTO control is behind and to the left of the operator's seat. (Yeah, right, really convenient!) On my WD, it's in front of the operator, but down between his feet. On the C, it's a lever under the operator's right leg, precisely where it can be confused with the belt pulley control. On the WC, it's a pull-rod way up low and forward under the throttle and behind the steering wheel pedestal. On Linda's John Deere B, it's beside the right foot—there are two levers there, so be sure you get the right one. The PTO engagement lever is the one closest to the gear shift lever. On the CA it's behind the operator, and to the right, where it's almost impossible to reach while you're operating the tractor. You'd think someone would have made up his mind about the best location for this control at some point along the line, but that has not happened so far. It has always been a matter, apparently, of the engineers saying, "Oops. We forgot a control for the PTO. Hmmm . . . Well, let's just stick it *here!*"

A handy addition to a PTO, usually bought and installed by the tractor owner rather than attached at the factory by the manufacturer, is an OVERRUNNING CLUTCH. This device is installed between the PTO and the shaft, carrying the power to the equipment it is driving. An overrunning clutch prohibits the rotation of the equipment from being carried back to the tractor transmission when the tractor stops. If you are, for example, cutting brush or stalks with a shredder (that is, a mower), when you stop the tractor, the rotation of the heavy blades of the shredder will continue to drive the tractor forward, a very dangerous situation obviously. You don't want that. When you want a tractor to stop, you want it to stop. An overrunning clutch helps you do that.

Okay, we've taken some detours here on our path following the tractor motor's power on its way to the rear wheels, but now let's get back on that track. The rotation of the driveshaft passes through a GEARBOX somewhere along here. Out of the gearbox sticks a lever, the GEAR SHIFT

LEVER, which allows the operator to select a variety of GEARS that give the drive wheels the power in various degrees of speed and force to move the entire tractor down the road or furrow. (There is sometimes a small thumb lever on the gear shift lever, the REVERSE LATCH, that, when depressed, allows the operator to shift the tractor into reverse and prevents accidental shifting into this gear. You can imagine the trouble that might occur if you were cruising along in road gear happily whistling and admiring the countryside, came to a hill, and, intending to shift into a lower gear, accidentally shifted into reverse. I think you would probably stop whistling pretty quickly.)

Inside the gearbox are, well, a bunch of gears. The lever in your hand moves a series of gears in the box by means of little metal ears and arms on shafts called SHIFTER LUGS and SHIFTER FORKS to move the gears back and forth on or with shafts. With various combinations, the rotation and power of the engine and driveshaft are translated into higher speeds of the shaft back of the gears (but with less power) or lower speeds (but with more power). If you know anything at all about an automobile, you understand how this trade off between speed and power works, or you know that it *does* work whether you understand it or not. Modern automatic gear shifts usually have a drive gear and a park, maybe a low gear, and, of course, a reverse. Tractors are more likely to have numbered gears, with 1 as the lowest gear, and 3 or 4 as the highest gears on an older tractor. More about that in a minute.

Most old-tractor transmissions aren't SYNCHRONIZED to allow you simply to depress the clutch and shift into another gear. You may have to start off in whatever gear you need and then slip the clutch—that is, let the clutch out slowly as the tractor starts moving—until you get up to speed and the clutch is completely out, or engaged. Some tractors allow or require DOUBLE CLUTCHING, depressing the clutch, shifting into neutral, releasing the clutch, increasing the motor speed and thus also the gear speed with the throttle, quickly depressing the clutch again, and shifting gently into the higher gear. This is pretty clumsy, as you can imagine, but race cars often require double clutching. So, if you have to go through all this with your tractor, just pretend that you're driving a Formula One or Indy race car instead and enjoy yourself.

If you have only driven an automatic-transmission automobile, you may never have encountered any gear system other than D for drive, R for reverse, and P for park. Old-timers will think I'm nuts for bothering to tell you this bit of information, but I know that my own 40-year-old children probably don't know this, so here it comes. First gear (1) is low, the slowest but most powerful gearing; second (2) is faster but not as powerful; third gear (3) is even faster but less powerful, and so on. Various tractors have different numbers of forward gears or speeds and sadly, one can't be sure where the gear shift lever needs to go to get into any particular gear since they have different arrangements. The good news is that there is usually a diagram of exactly where the lever needs to go to find any particular gear on the casting that the gear shift lever goes into to reach the gears themselves.

A couple of terms that come up when discussing tractor gearing are ROAD GEAR, usually a fast-speed gear that lets the operator move quickly on open ground when the tractor is not pulling or driving auxiliary equipment, and GRANNY LOW or TRACTOR LOW, an extremely low gear that moves the tractor at a very slow speed, sometimes no faster than a slow walk, but with very high power.

Some tractors like my International 300 Utility tractor have a TORQUE AMPLIFIER that uses another gearing system to lower all the gears of the tractor down a notch to give it more power, and less speed. (TORQUE is the twisting or rotating power of any turning device.) If your tractor has a torque amplifier, you can almost surely count on the lever for it being broken off. For some reason, they always are.

From the gearbox, the rotation of the drive system—which is to say the power that can be used to drive equipment—continues toward the drive wheels of the tractor, which are almost always the large, heavy, rear wheels of the machine. (This is in contrast to modern automobiles like my Ford Taurus where the drive wheels are often the front wheels and all the wheels of the vehicle are the same size.) Sometimes mechanisms for powering equipment are located behind the gearbox—lifts, pulleys, drives—but usually not, since this arrangement would require the tractor to be in motion to provide auxiliary power.

Now the driveshaft—usually within a heavy metal case that may actually be the entire body of the tractor at this point, called the TORQUE TUBE—continues to the REAR END. Once at the rear end, the shaft enters the DIFFERENTIAL where REAR AXLES residing at right angles to the driveshaft split the torque (drive) to the rear drive wheels. I wish I could tell you how the differential works, but for the life of me I've never been able to understand it myself even though I've tried now for 50 years. I've looked at diagrams, even examined working models of differential systems, but I still don't get it. I don't know what to tell you, other than thank goodness someone does understand differentials. I do know that if the rear wheels were rigidly attached to a single solid AXLE (the heavy rod on which the wheels are mounted), one of the wheels would be dragged along at every corner the tractor turned, insuring ferocious wear on the tires and plenty of discomfort for the operator. A system of gears in the large case where the driveshaft links with the rear axle somehow—miraculously, as far as I can tell—compensates for this problem and delivers the power to the axles and out to the rear drive wheels with allowance for this difference; hence, differential.

Sometimes, as with a John Deere B for example, the axles extend directly from the differential to the middle of the rear wheels. On other tractors like my Allises, the axle drives a large gear, the BULL GEAR, which then engages a gear on the true axle or spindle at the outer extreme of the rear and to which each rear wheel is bolted. This last transfer of power is called the FINAL DRIVE.

Because of the way a tractor works—pulling heavy equipment over uneven, soft ground—one of the most visible and consistent features of a tractor is its large, sometimes *huge*, back wheels.

Some tractors called CRAWLERS move on TRACKS like a tank. They are usually steered with levers or pedals rather than a steering wheel. These are relatively rare (although interesting) compared to wheeled machines. Since I am not at all familiar with crawlers, I'm not going to try to tell you much about the mechanisms where they differ from the conventional, wheeled tractor. I will note that since they are rare and interesting, they are consistently also the most expensive antique tractors on the market. I sure wish I had one!

As I advise you so often in these pages, for information about specific tractors, the best thing to do is to obtain a manual, guide, or parts book for it. Or better yet, find an old-timer who knows his stuff about this particular machine and who is willing to sit down and share his knowledge with you. If you put a little effort into it, this shouldn't be hard, and certainly not impossible. The hard part, you'll find, is getting your old-timer tractor guru to stop talking once you get him started.

The rear WHEELS vary considerably in size and form from tractor to tractor. They are steel, sometimes solid disks, sometimes with heavy weights bolted on them to provide added TRACTION for the drive wheels by putting more weight on that part of the machine that touches and pushes on the ground to move forward. Sometimes the wheels have SPOKES, square or round rods that hold the wheel's rim to the HUB, the central point of the wheel into which the axle slides. Tractor veterans can tell a lot from a tractor wheel's spokes. On my Allis WCs, for example, square-spoked wheels are usually old steel-wheeled tractors that have had the old lugged rims cut off and rims for rubber tires welded on. This was so common that even small rural and small-town shops became skilled enough at this operation that you can scarcely tell them from factory-produced wheels. On an old Allis, round spokes are a sign of a factory-produced rubber tire wheel.

Sometimes tractor wheels have arrangements by which the distance between the rear wheels—the POWER ADJUST WHEEL—can be adjusted to permit mounting of different equipment or to fit the wheels into the furrows made by various pieces of equipment without damaging crops. At least theoretically, every power-adjust wheel I've seen on an unrestored old tractor has been frozen solidly in place, just as it has been for at least the past 20 years.

On Linda's John Deere B, the spacing between the rear wheels can be adjusted by sliding the entire wheel in or out on the fluted (or "splined") end of the rear axle. This may not seem like a particularly important piece of information, but it is painfully and indelibly etched in my mind. I bought Linda her JD B as a Christmas present. It was beautifully restored and nicely painted by my pal, Dick, and delivered right to our farm, where I put a big red ribbon on it and invited Linda out from the house to see her new toy. She was happy, I was happy, Dick was happy. End of story, right? Not quite.

As we stood there in the yard admiring the tractor, a storm came up. I sure didn't want to see that new paint job damaged, so I decided to run the tractor into my shop, which was empty at the time. I started it and headed out the gate and around to the shop, all the while mumbling to myself the standard John Deere B mantra, "Hand clutch. Hand clutch. Hand clutch." You see, my Allises all have foot clutches, even if they also have a hand clutch, and I had been regaled for years with stories about guys like me—who were not used to the John Deere hand clutch—driving through the back of barns while madly flailing with their feet trying to disengage the motor before the tractor destroyed itself *and* the barn. I was not going to make that mistake with this pretty tractor of Linda's.

I rounded the corner and carefully approached the open front door of the shop, my hand resting confidently on that accursed hand clutch. Yep, I was no dummy. I was completely ready to pull that thing and disengage the motor smartly, also knowing that the very same hand lever operated the tractor's brakes. "Hand clutch. Hand clutch. Hand clutch."

All I can remember now about the event is the horrifying noise of splintering wood and the cloud of rubble and ruin that collapsed on and around me as I passed through the shop door. As I got the tractor stopped, got off, and pulled away all the wreckage of insulation, sheetrock, plywood, and two-by-fours that had been the door frame, I also remembered another important thing about John Deere Bs—the axles of a John Deere B stick out a good 6 inches on either side of the wheels for adjustment of the wheel base. Oh yeah. I haven't ever forgotten that little piece of information again.

The RIM of a wheel is the outside flange onto which the TIRES are mounted; you will often see an old-timer looking at a tractor he is thinking of buying and shaking his head at the rear wheels. Tractor tires are sometimes filled with a liquid—a brine—that adds a lot more weight right where it is needed, where the rubber hits the ground. If this liquid leaks from the tire onto the rim at any point, it is almost certain to corrode the rim. That is why old tractor wheels are hard to find and painfully expensive. It is also why antique tractor enthusiasts are constantly shopping around for other liquids to put in their tractor tires, from antifreeze to kerosene, each bringing along its own unique complications to the equation. This was not a custom with tractors before the 1940s, so you may never run into it with truly antique tractors. The subject may come up, so I thought I'd give you fair warning just in case.

Rubber tires are something of a recent development for tractors. If you look around at a tractor show or museum, you will almost certainly find an old tractor on STEEL. Steel tractor wheels are intimidating things, looking for all the world like something off a medieval siege machine, or maybe from a science-fiction battle engine. Instead of a rubber tire like the modern wheel and tire arrangement, there is nothing but steel, with large heavy spikes or LUGS, also referred to as SPADES, attached to dig in for traction. As you can imagine, this arrangement made a lot of sense for farmers, or at least it seemed to. The lugs dug into the ground and gave the tractor absolute traction. But one thing you may have already noticed about old tractors is that they don't have a suspension system like an automobile: no springs, shock absorbers, padded seats on springs, nothing! To put it bluntly, there is nothing but iron between the operator's rear end and a rock lying in the path of those rear wheels.

I once drove a tractor on steel and lugs the mile from my farm into town, driving along the ditch until I got to the first street in town. In that short one-mile drive, I felt every single cigarette butt and aluminum can lying in my path, right up through the iron wheels, up the axle, into the frame, up the iron mount for the iron seat, and directly to my butt. It took me two weeks to stop stuttering after that drive. I cannot imagine spending days on a steel-wheeled tractor working a rocky field. Man, the only thing that stopped me on that trip was when I hit the gravel streets in town. When I saw the damage I was doing by tearing up the town's streets with my tractor's lugs, I understood for the first time in my life the signs I'd seen along roads and highways as a kid: "OIL ROAD—TRACTORS WITH LUGS PROHIBITED." I decided that if I didn't want a visit from the town marshal, I better turn that tractor around and head back down the ditch toward home.

I was later advised by some old-timer friends of mine that all I needed to do was get that tractor into road gear at about 15 miles an hour and the lugs would skim right along on top of the ground. Uh-huh, sure, 15 miles per hour! On steel wheels with lugs, 15 miles per hour. Oh yeah. It stands to reason, however, that an old-fashioned farmer in 1934 or 1935 took one look at those soft, relatively slick, new-fangled *rubber* tires, and then at his *steel-lug* wheels and figured those steel wheels were dang-sure going to give him better traction than rubber while spring plowing in the soft dirt of a cornfield! Not to mention that rubber tires on his Model A Ford automobile went flat every hundred miles or so. Well, there wasn't the slightest chance in ruby-red hell that his steelies with cast-iron lugs were going to go flat on him! Nope, he wasn't going to take that kind of chance and invest in those new-fangled rubber-band balloon tires for *his* tractor.

Believe it or not, it was Allis-Chalmers and Goodyear who turned that trend around with about as clever a publicity stunt as you can imagine, worthy of the smartest and slickest of today's Madison Avenue hucksters. They got the famous race car driver Barney Oldfield to crawl up onto the seat of a souped-up Allis-Chalmers tractor with rubber tires—I think it was a U model—and run it around the track at Indianapolis at over 60 miles per hour! Imagine that: driving a tractor at more than 60 miles per hour! That day Oldfield earned whatever they paid him. But the stunt worked. It convinced farmers of the safety and efficiency of rubber tires, and the era of steel wheels slowly ground to a jarring end. Today, steel-lugged wheels are only a novelty seen at exhibits and antique tractor shows.

There are many kinds of steel wheels, by the way. My steel-wheeled Allis came on heavy rims with a double row of lugs, but I also have a set of SPIDER WHEELS or TIPTOE WHEELS, light steel frame works with lugs attached along thin but strong rails. I also have a monstrous set of wheels with very heavy rims and lugs that appear to be homemade. I suspect that there were a lot of these such things welded and bolted together by individual farmers across the countryside and they probably still lie rusting underneath piles of straw, lumber, and manure in abandoned barns around America. Before moving wrecked tractors into my shop for the two-year job of rebuilding them, I take off the old, rotten, stinking, dirty, clumsy, big rubber tires and replace them with a set of old steel wheels from which I have removed the lugs. This enables me to move the tractor more easily and saves me a lot of room and mess in the shop. See? Those old iron wheels do still have a practical purpose.

Rear rubber tires came over the years in many forms and sometimes an old tractor shows up for sale or show with what might strike you as an unusually treaded tire. These are KNOBBIES, which, as the name suggests, had round rubber knobs instead of the more usual modern tread with slanted rubber bars. Originally, I am told, my Allises came on Goodyear tires with a diamond-shaped tread. Today, almost all rubber tires have the chevron pattern of raised bars standard to modern tractor tires, but be careful! There is a front way and back way for them, and if you should have the misfortune to mount them backwards, you are sure going to hear about it! When the tire is properly mounted on the tractor, the bottom point of the V of the tread on top of the rotation should point toward the front of the tractor.

The rear wheels are mounted to the hub with LUG NUTS, large steel nuts attached to studs protruding from the HUB, or, in the case of some tractors like Linda's John Deere B, by a single, large HUB NUT fitted to and turning onto the threaded axle.

The front wheels of a tractor are less imposing than the back. They are much smaller and usually have parallel ribs running lengthwise around the outside. The wheels simply rotate on short axles so there is no driving mechanism attached to them. They just contain bearings and seals, terms I will discuss later. They simply roll along as the back wheels drive the tractor, providing no power of their own. The hub nuts, seals, and bearings are often covered with a grease cup called the HUBCAP. The spacing of the front wheels of a tractor is usually adjusted by turning one or both of them around on the axle (there is no forward or backward to the front tires as there is for the rear).

CHAPTER 3

FRAME AND
SHEET METAL

This is going to be a short section of the book. As you can see with even the most casual glance, there isn't a lot of sheet metal or frame to an old tractor. In fact, on some of the old machines sitting around here, there is no frame at all. The main structure of the tractor is not like a car, which has a bunch of supports and skin to hold everything together and up off the ground. In the case of many old tractors, the frame is actually nothing more than the steering mechanism. The engine, the torque tube, clutch housing, gearboxes, and the rear end and wheels are all lined up and bolted together to form a so-called INTEGRAL or

INTEGRATED FRAME. Everything else is hung onto that. In short, the tractor parts and housings *are* the machine's frame. To get at the motor or transmission, no kidding, you have to BREAK the tractor—that is, block up the middle and detach the front of the machine from the back. My Allis C is like that. The sheetmetal skin on such a machine makes a very small pile indeed! Tractors are fundamentally *tools* and there's not a lot of allowance for the vanity of fancy sheetmetal cosmetics.

On the other hand, my Allis G is mostly frame: a lot of struts and structure with an engine mounted on the back and wheels sort of stuck on at the corners. My favorite tractors, Allis WCs, offer a nice compromise. Along each side from the rear axle to the front steering pedestal there are two heavy beams, the SIDE BEAMS, which are attached to give the tractor added strength and provide mounting points for steering, control pedals, the belt pulley, and other mechanisms. Best of all for guys like me who are working on the machine, this lets us pull the motor or drop the front steering pedestal without having to break the tractor—that is, actually take apart the front and rear parts of the tractor from each other.

Let's take a look at the parts of what might be considered an old tractor's frame, starting from the front PEDESTAL. The pedestal is the large, very heavy metal casting that houses the steering components.

On the front frame of some tractors there are various MOUNTS for attaching farming equipment and tools like hoists, lifts, and buckets. In fact, you can find mounts just about anywhere on any particular tractor! It seems folks were hanging stuff all over tractors, and they probably still do. The principal place to find HITCHES, mounts, hooks, and holes is somewhere along the back of the tractor, where the most straight forward power can be applied to it, somewhere near the power take-off, back where the operator can keep an eye on it without being constantly in the cloud of dust generated by the equipment. The most common and safest site for attaching things from plows and cultivators to chains and ropes is the DRAWBAR at the back of the tractor, usually right behind and below the operator's seat. The drawbar is a very heavy bar of steel, sometimes running across the back of the tractor almost from wheel to wheel. You'll find a series of holes on the drawbar that can be used to connect a variety of attachments. You will probably also see a SNAP-COUPLER, TWO-POINT, THREE-POINT, SPEED, FAST, or QUICK HITCH at the rear of a tractor, sometimes incorporating, grouped around, or connected with the drawbar. These hitches are what allow you to hook up your implements. Some, like the Snap-Coupler and Fast Hitch are systems developed by specific manufacturers to speed up the attaching of machinery to a tractor, in this case, International and Allis-Chalmers. Others, like the three-point hitch, while developed by a single manufacturer, have become standards for the field.

Not to confuse you, but you may also see somewhere around there a swinging or fixed drawbar, which is a single heavy steel pole coming back along the frame or under the rear end. At the end of the drawbar, farthest away from the tractor frame, resides a single hole into which a heavy pin, hitch, spindle, or CLEVIS can be put. (A clevis is a U-or twisted U-shaped piece of heavy steel that can be quickly and easily attached to the drawbar by dropping a heavy pin through two holes, one at each end of the clevis and through a hole in the drawbar.) It sounds complicated, but just ask someone standing near a tractor where the drawbar is, he'll point at it, and you will instantly understand what I'm trying to tell you in far too many words.

Two-point, three-point, and speed hitches are various systems engineered by tractor manufacturers for the quick, safe, and secure mounting of equipment on a tractor. Such hitches also manipulate the equipment, generally not much more than by raising and lowering it, usually hydraulically but sometimes mechanically. Arms or receptacles on the back of the tractor allow equipment to be quickly attached and controlled, always with the hope that the operator wouldn't have to get out of his seat and down off the tractor to attach the equipment any more often than necessary. This was a great aspiration, but it was only rarely met as any veteran farmer will tell you. Regardless of the type of labor-saving hitch, mounting equipment usually was—and still is—a two-person job.

Perhaps the least important part of a tractor's frame, certainly and obviously in the minds of the people who designed and engineered tractors, is the place where the operator sits. This has to be one of the real wonders of tractor design. How did the manufacturers think the operator was supposed to get up to the seat, much less sit in it? If any thought was ever given by a manufacturer to the comfort of the poor guy who had to run that tractor across fields for long hours and long days at a time, it sure isn't evident. If you are a newcomer to the world of old tractors, your first question is sure to be, "How the heck do you get up on this thing?" There are no handholds, no steps, no easy access. The people who designed and built these things just assumed you'd figure out a way, and so it's pretty much up to you. Step on the drawbar and then onto the PTO shield, get up on the hydraulics reservoir, throw your leg over the back of the seat, step on the transmission, grab onto the overhead loader support frame, swing both feet (one at a time!) over the steering wheel or seat, put one leg between the hand clutch and the steering shaft, wiggle your other foot down onto the brake pedal, and . . . ha! There you are! Don't waste a lot of time looking for an easy way to get up to that seat; there really isn't one.

Nor does the seat offer much comfort for the operator. On an old tractor, the seat is more often than not made out of iron, plain and simple, bolted to 2 feet of solid steel strap with about as much give as Mount Rushmore. Old tractor seats are usually shaped to precisely fit the bottom of a largish farmer in such a way that it will launch him up out into the middle of the field after he runs over an unusually firm clod while crossing an open field.

I love the Allis WCs and WDs, with their wonderfully pathetic gesture toward an easy ride with their seats mounted onto a hinge and placed directly over a big ol' spring with a shock absorber in the middle. It's still for all the world like riding something at a carnival. My Allis C has a BENCH SEAT, a nice, wide flat seat with a foam-filled pad. Of course that is the *only* cushioning between your bum and the pavement, but it was a nice thought on the part of the designer.

The seat is usually placed directly behind the exhaust stack and in the path of the hot, stinky gases exiting the motor so that your face will get the full impact of it all. I think that's to keep your nose warm in the winter. Controls are placed just out of reach, and if there are two that might be engaged by your hands at the same moment, they will be at opposite sides of the machine. On my WCs, for example, while you are driving with both hands flailing on the steering wheel, you will also find yourself using your hands to operate the brakes, two levers on either side of the rear of the tractor, which are a good 5 feet apart. Then the hand throttle is smack in the middle. On a WD, you steer while operating the hand clutch, hand throttle, and hand choke, both cleverly placed in the middle of the steering wheel so you have to reach *through* the steering wheel to get to them.

I asked my friend Dick Day to check on this and make sure I had it right. I think his response says worlds about exactly how right I am: "Rog, the PTO lever is at the base of the steering pedestal, just an inch or two from the brake pedal. I sat up there to see what it would take for me to pull it up. Pretty much, my face was in the steering wheel. If only I had ape arms . . ."

Of course, tractors are to this day designed for one operator and no passengers. If you should want to carry a passenger, well, God help them, and be sure you have a big liability insurance policy in place. It is very dangerous to put anyone on a fender, or even dumber, the hood, of a tractor. You may find a possible perch on the back, but even that has its hazards. I once needed some help and decided it was time to teach my then nine-year-old daughter Joyce how to drive Sweet Allis. It should be simple enough, after all, since you set the throttle and don't really have to worry about much of anything but steering. In an emergency, you can pull on just one brake and get the thing stopped or turning in a tight circle, right?

Okay, so I stood on the little rear platform over the PTO shaft and was showing her the few things she needed to know to help me out that day, helped her put it in gear, showed her how to slooooooooowly let out the clutch. I could see the disaster coming from a mile away. Her skinny little leg was extended as far as it could go, not only out in front of her but at a crazy angle to the left—another feature of the genius design of the Allis WC. There was no way she was going to be able to ease that clutch out. No way!

And she didn't. It snapped out, the tractor lurched forward, I was thrown off the back and onto the ground. Joyce and Sweet Allis went across our pastureland utterly out of control. She was going slowly enough that there was no danger, but by the time I got up off the ground, there was also no chance of me catching her. She was screaming bloody murder and I can tell you for a fact that an Allis WC tractor—they don't use silly little sissy things like mufflers on their exhaust system—is anything but quiet even without a screaming little girl at the controls. I finally yelled to her to turn the wheel and got her going in a circle so I could get close to her. Waving my arms frantically, running alongside her sort of, I conveyed my instructions to pull back on the throttle to slow it down to a speed that I could maybe match with my short legs. I then managed to catch her and finally kill the motor.

To my knowledge, Joyce has never again in all her life gotten back up on a tractor.

Now, the following may seem like a really silly thing to include in this book, much less stick into a chapter on the tractor's frame, and yet it may be the most important item of all for the serious antique tractor collector or restorer—*the tractor's serial number!* The thing is, a tractor's serial number can tell you when that tractor was manufactured, and that is crucial information for a dyed-in-the-wool tractor nut. Automobiles vary—even if only slightly, even if ridiculously—from year to year and someone who cares about that kind of thing can look at a car and tell you what year it rolled off the assembly line. The same tractor model is made for years, even decades, with no easily discernable differences. So to tell what year a tractor was made, you need to find that serial number.

I'd love to tell you where to find that serial number, but I can't. The location varies from tractor to tractor, even model to model. The best thing you can do is get your hands on a general serial number guide for tractors, or a guide for your tractor in particular. Again, I recommend Jensales, which publishes a comprehensive guide to tractor serial numbers *and* their locations from model to model.

To complicate things even further, you may also find a serial number on a tractor's motor or transmission, which probably has nothing or little to do with the actual *tractor's* serial number. Nobody promised you this would be simple.

As for a tractor's sheet metal, or bodywork, a tractor is a stripped down, motorized tool without a lot of time, patience, or allowance made for fripperies. When you are on a tractor, you are on the no-frills trip of your life, and that goes for sheet metal too. Only rarely is the skin of a tractor put there to be pretty. It protects a few parts from the weather, wear, and that's about it. That's the way most old-tractor nuts like it, too. There are two models of the Allis-Chalmers WC (and this goes for many

other makes of tractor too), UNSTYLED and—ooooh, fancy-dansy!
—STYLED. I have a couple of styled examples sitting around here, but I am
not all that proud of them. The difference between styled and unstyled is
actually not very dramatic: there is a rounded, "streamlined" COWLING
covering the radiator on the styled model. The unstyled version just has
that square old radiator sitting out there unadorned and unpretending.
The unstyled model has a squarish gas tank that is clearly nothing more
than a gas tank. The styled model has a "bullet" tank that makes the
tractor look silly because exactly how much streamlining do you need
when you're pulling a manure spreader across a field at 2 miles an hour?

Finally, the FENDERS of the unstyled Allis are square shields that
weigh about as much as a modern automobile and wouldn't show a dent
or ding if you whacked them with a sledgehammer. You can rest your right
hand comfortably on an unstyled fender, or sit a kid up there for a scary
ride, at least until her mother sees you and chews you out for putting the
kid's life in danger. (The child, on the other hand, will carry memories of
that ride with the stinking exhaust in her face well into her maturity as a
treasure of her youth.) On the styled model, there are CLAMSHELL fenders
that let the tires throw mud into the air, onto you, and anyone behind you.
They leave you no place to rest a Braunschweiger sandwich at noon, and
they twist and bend in a good breeze.

I guess you can tell my prejudices when it comes to styled and
unstyled sheet metal.

A tractor HOOD isn't much either, it's usually not much more than
a sheet of flat metal that keeps the rain off the motor when the machine

is parked. Unlike automobiles, a tractor hood doesn't swing open at the flick of a latch and a lift of the hand. It is usually bolted down and has to be unfastened to be removed, but that's okay because on most old tractors the entire engine is open to inspection, repair, and servicing without removing the hood. You only take the hood off when something really serious needs to be done, like working on the valves or replacing a water pump.

On some tractors there are SKIRTS and/or specialized SHIELDS, bits of sheet metal, often louvered, that are attached or hung from hooks and latches along the sides of the engine. These are designed to protect tractor parts when working with dirty work like picking corn or potentially dangerous jobs like orchard work where branches might damage motor parts or the radiator. These parts were usually set aside, and lost eventually, so they tend to be rare items, eagerly sought after and dearly paid for by tractor restorers.

Very few antique tractors had a CAB, or enclosed compartment for the operator. That's why the old image of the farmer in the past was a man with sunburned nape of the neck, a red nose, and a white forehead. There were some temporary enclosures called HEAT CABS that were meant to protect the tractor operator from wind and even funnel some motor heat back to them while working during the winter. Since these were usually made of fragile canvas and exposed to the elements, not many have survived for restoration.

I have saved the most important feature of the tractor's skin for the end of this section: the PAINT! It's not that the paint is all that important in the performance of the tractor, or in its durability, or even in the restoration. If you've spent any time at all with an old-tractor nut, or better yet several old-tractor nuts, then you know that the color of a tractor is not a matter of passing interest.

Thing is, you can buy a silver Ford automobile, or a black one. You can own a red Pontiac, or a green one, or a blue one. You can buy just about any automobile in colors you can't even identify. Our current car, a Ford Taurus, is champagne colored—a kind of silver-gray-brown. Automobile owners argue about horsepower, comfort, miles per gallon, safety, even speed, but you're not likely to find yourself in a heated argument among automobile owners about the *color* of their cars.

Not so with tractors and tractor owners. All John Deeres are green and all Allis-Chalmers are orange. The Allis-Chalmers are not just *any* orange, but *Persian* orange. Internationals are red and Fords are gray, and so it goes. When you hear someone talking about a tractor show called "The Gathering of the Green," you don't have to ask what kind of tractors you'll see there. You'll see John Deeres, and that's for sure. But you won't see a lot of Deeres at a Gathering of the Orange or a Gathering of the Red!

You'll see tractor collectors dressed completely in green, wearing lapel pins saying "Friends don't let friends drive red tractors." And you'll hear that John Deeres are green so no one will see them when the weeds grow up around their dead carcasses when they finally give up and die. I consider myself a lover of old iron in general. I have said and written that a lot of times that it really isn't a matter of one tractor being any better than another, it's simply that we all love all old tractors. My peace-making, diplomatic, dovish, pacifist efforts notwithstanding, I am constantly identified as "that Allis-Chalmers guy," and I have to stand there and listen to jokes and insults from people wearing green coats or red caps no matter how much I protest.

Now, the second most important thing for a newcomer to the World of Old Tractors to know is that for all this fuss and feathers about tractor paint colors, it is nothing more than a bluff. No one—and I mean no one—really takes all this color and make competition seriously. For all the posturing and joking, at any gathering of old-tractor lovers, no matter what color cap or jacket they might be wearing, there is a pervasive and warm feeling of goodwill and camaraderie. No kidding. Even if you are completely dressed in red and have International patches, pins, and emblems covering you from head to toe, if you should run into trouble, say, unloading your tractor or need some help with anything from a nasty cut on your finger to a bit of gasoline to get your machine started, you can just go right ahead and ask the folks all in orange or green. No matter how loyal they may be to their favorite brand of tractor, the bottom line is that we all belong to the same fraternity, the one whose colors are rust.

So be prepared to defend your colors and take a lot of kidding about it, but don't go into such a discussion armed, not even with good arguments or stern words.

If I felt as if I were going out on a limb to talk about the color of a tractor's paint here, now I'm going to go one step further (and then stop, I promise) by adding one brief note about the decals on the paint of the tractor's sheet metal or on the tractor's frame. The first couple times you kibitz on a conversation between old-tractor lovers, it's going to sound like code to you:

"Does your friend Ralph still have that H he was so proud of?"

"Nah, he got rid of that and went to a 300."

"He always told me he was going to switch to an orange U or UC if he ever got the chance. You know he had his eye on both an 8N and an 88."

"That was all flapdoodle, I think, just to give Frank the idea that he wasn't really all that interested in that D14 . . ."

And on and on and on.

Automobile manufacturers give their cars names like Cougar, Taurus, Bearcat, or Lakota. They name their car models like most people name their kids—with no application of brainpower whatsoever. The only intelligent automobile name I've ever encountered is Lamborghini's Countach, a French colloquial idiom meaning roughly "*holy shit!*" If you have ever seen a Lamborghini Countach, you know why it is called that —because those were the first words out of your mouth upon seeing one.

Tractor manufacturers have a different system for designating their models, and I think this is the first time it has ever been revealed to the public. Manufacturers throw a whole bunch of pieces of paper with numbers and letters on them into someone's hat and then draw one out. Or maybe they draw out a number and a letter. And if two are stuck together, all the better. Whatever they pull out is what they name their next tractor model. Thus, we have the Allis-Chalmers U, UC, WC, WD, WD-14, C, B, CA, blah blah blah. (Although, I should note that my Lovely Linda says she always thought the "WC" in Allis-Chalmers WC stands for

"Welsch's Compulsion.") There is a common belief among tractor lovers that there will eventually be an Allis-Chalmers Size 7 1/8, or maybe a Ford Two Loaves of Bread, One Pound of Sugar, and a Tube of Toothpaste if someone accidentally drops a grocery shopping list into the hat.

It's completely nuts. Don't try to figure it out. And don't be surprised by anything. Believe it or not, there actually is a Farmall Super BM. I want one. I want one bad. Wouldn't it be a conversation stopper up at the town café to be able to announce loudly that you have never had anything but a Super BM? Or to say that morning you picked up a Super BM at an auction sale? Or that the only thing you want as you get along in life is a Super BM? I know that I, for one, admire a man with a Super BM. Some increasingly envy a man with a Super BM.

As you can see, the possibilities are endless. I have a John Deere B that has never started without my putting less than a full day's work into getting it going. I call it a John Deere SOB.

CHAPTER 4

FLUIDS

There are usually three principal systems in a tractor that transport fluids: the fuel system, the oil system, and the cooling system. As mentioned earlier, some tractor tires have fluid in them (calcium chloride, by the way, which is a form of salt), but that doesn't really count because it just sits there in the tires doing nothing more than providing weight, kind of like me at an opera. Newer tractors have hydraulic systems using a fluid—usually a petroleum-based oil to carry force and power to various auxiliary units on the tractor, implements, tools, or machines.

Now, there are other minor fluids involved with tractors too. For example, if a tractor has a battery, there's battery acid in it, and a later-model machine may have hydraulic brakes, which started to show up in the 1950s and 1960s, but basically older tractor fluids boil down to coolant, oil, and fuel.

A few tractors have air-cooled motors. Dave Mowitz, *Successful Farming's* agricultural machinery whiz and tractor guru tells me that the German company Deutz made—and still makes—air-cooled tractor motors. According to Dave, some were installed in Allis exports to this country. The vast majority of tractor motors use a coolant circulating through the engine's water jacket by means of a pump or convection. Some older manuals and guides refer to this as "thermosiphon," but the term didn't stick apparently since "convection" is now the standard term. The coolant—usually water with an antifreeze added—also passes through a device that carries the heat from it and disperses it into the air: a RADIATOR. While some older tractors used convection to move coolant, most tractors utilize a PUMP. Driven by either a gear or a belt, a water pump moves coolant more quickly and certainly through the block's WATER JACKET—the space around the cylinders—and radiator than the convection method.

Water or coolant may not seem like a particularly important thing, since it doesn't really make a motor *go*, but in a bad situation, I'd rather run out of gasoline than water. Fuel burning in a motor's cylinders runs around 4,500 degrees Fahrenheit. That's hot. Especially if you consider that iron melts at about 2,500 degrees. Hmmm . . . your motor is made of iron, which melts at 2,500 degrees, but you have a constant series of fires going on inside that run almost twice that hot. It is the coolant that keeps that engine from melting down. If you run out of gas, the motor just stops. If you run out of coolant and ignore that fact too long, your motor starts melting around the edges and seizes up. See? Coolant is important.

A FAN is mounted somewhere behind the radiator, often to the pump itself. The fan forces air through the radiator to carry off the excess heat of the coolant, even if the tractor is not moving through the air, such as when it is stationary, idling, or perhaps running a piece of stationary equipment like a mill or buzz saw.

By the way, antifreeze can be dangerous stuff. In the old days, they used alcohol to keep the motor and radiator from freezing up and breaking under the pressure of the ice. Now modern antifreezes are usually based on glycol, a form of sugar. The glycol makes it kind of sweet tasting, which is a dangerous temptation to animals like dogs and cats, especially because it *is* toxic enough to kill. Be careful with antifreeze is the moral of *that* story! In the old days, some daredevils actually used kerosene in their tractors' cooling systems as the coolant. The hot kerosene was not all that far from the fires in the cylinder, and the occasional accidental spark from the electrical system. Hmmm. Since one of my grandfathers died in a kerosene explosion, I think I'm going to pass on the notion of using an explosive liquid as antifreeze, thank you very much!

The cooling system on a motor is a mixed blessing. Sure, you want to carry excess heat away from the cylinders and block when the motor is humming along and everything is warmed up nicely. But when you *start* that machine, especially in cold weather, you *want* it to warm up quickly so the fuel burns easily in the cylinders and oil flows more easily over the moving parts. So, what can you do to help the motor warm up quickly in the beginning, and yet stay cool when it is working hard for you at full load?

There are a couple of answers to that on old tractors. Perhaps the earliest and most primitive was a set of SHUTTERS set right in front of the radiator, usually behind the grill, since this adjustable lattice work tended to be a little fragile, especially during rigorous agricultural work. Shutters are like Venetian blinds, but they are usually vertical when used as a tractor part. A lever, usually operated from the operator's position on the tractor, opened and closed the shutters, allowing more or less air to pass through, over, and around the radiator and motor.

A similar alternative system for cutting off or slowing the airflow through the tractor's radiator and over the motor were CURTAINS, simple sheets of cloth that covered the intake side of the radiator. A curtain can be on a roller like a window shade, pulled down over the radiator's front while the motor warms up, or even more simply a cover that is detachable or folded up by hand once the motor is warm.

An automatic and less fragile tool for the same purpose is a THERMOSTAT. This very simple valve is installed in the cooling system, typically in the radiator hose, on the water manifold at the block, head, or radiator. It closes when the coolant is cool, thus preventing coolant from circulating through the block and radiator. Conversely, it opens as the coolant warms up, thus letting the coolant do its job of cooling. The temperature of the fluid in the tractor's cooling system is sometimes indicated for the operator by a gauge placed on a control panel near the operator's station, but sometimes it is located elsewhere. On my Allis WCs, the temperature gauge is on the top of the radiator at the front of the hood. However, usually it is somewhere where it can be seen. If the coolant is running too hot—more than boiling or 212 degrees Fahrenheit—you have trouble.

So, briefly, the liquid in the cooling system takes the heat away from the cylinders and the block, is pushed by the pump (often but not always) into a radiator where it transfers the heat to air passing over the heat-conducting metal (usually copper), and then is sent back into the motor to do that job all over again. In very rare cases, the water system may be used for other purposes too: in later-model tractors with cabs, the warmed coolant may also provide heat for a heating system. In a very few models, a water injection manifold spritzes water into the cylinders for added power. Generally speaking, it's a good idea for the coolant to stay right where it is in the cooling system, and it's especially unwelcome if it shows up in the fuel, oil, or hydraulic systems where it is nothing but trouble.

It's hard to imagine that something as gentle and benign as water can split open a solid, cast-iron hunk like a tractor's motor block, but I can tell you with very real tears in my eyes that it can. Ask any veteran mechanic and he'll tell you the same thing. If you are still a skeptic, fill a tin can with water and put it outside the next time it freezes. Or leave it in your freezer overnight. See?

Blocks sometimes have FREEZE PLUGS in them to prevent the enormous destruction freezing water can inflict on a motor. Freeze plugs are round plugs pushed firmly and tightly into openings made specifically for them in the side of the block's water jacket. If the motor should freeze up, the theory goes, the ice will push out the plugs before it cracks the block. Well, maybe, but that still isn't going to prevent damage to the radiator. Believe me, your best bet is to keep your tractor motors well provided with fresh, modern, commercial antifreeze. (A side benefit of modern antifreezes is that they also have lubricants in them for seals and pumps.)

If you can't do that, tractors have DRAIN PLUGS. If you don't have antifreeze in your tractor, or enough antifreeze to deal with intense cold, you can simply open the drain plugs and remove the coolant from the radiator and engine where it could potentially do damage. (Be sure to put drained antifreeze into closed containers!) And be sure you open *all* the drain plugs. A buddy once asked me to drain his tractor's cooling system before a hard freeze, but since that was before I knew even the simplest basics about tractors, I opened only the one at the base of the radiator. My friend was *not* pleased when he found that the coolant left in the motor had cracked the block.

We've already touched on the oil circulation system in the block, but it is worth reviewing. The oil in a motor lubricates all sorts of parts from the valves and rocker arm assembly to the main bearings and pistons. All too often we forget that the circulating oil also helps in cooling the block and carrying off the destructive elements of combustion and wear that are constantly going on in that block. Some of those nasties are exhausted elements and carbon that sneak past the pistons and piston rings; tiny bits of metal from the wear in the cylinders, in bearings, along guides and contact points like the tappets; and unburned fuel that can find its way past the combustion process, down into the crankcase, and around the valves. Not to mention all manner of other pollutants that can damage a motor and other oiled parts, especially with farm equipment that is constantly exposed to dust, dirt, moisture, and flying plant debris. I honestly believe that the best thing you can do to prolong the life of an engine, whether it's on a lawn mower, a tractor, an automobile, generator, or chain saw, is change the oil regularly. You aren't saving yourself any money by skimping on regular oil changes.

The oil in a tractor motor is drawn from the PAN or SUMP by a pump, pushed through lines into a filter and to parts of the engine that need lubrication. Oil usually passes up and over the valve rocker arms, pushrods, and tappets, and then back to the pan, where it is also splashed by the crankshaft journals up into the cylinder bottoms, onto the camshaft, etc. Somewhere along the line there may also be an OIL GAUGE to inform the operator if sufficient pressure is being generated by the pump to push oil where it is needed. Because of the importance of oil being pushed to all those moving parts, the gauge is usually somewhere within the operator's line of sight. If a tractor has a control panel near the operator's station, you will probably find the oil pressure gauge there. On my Allis WCs, it is at the oil filter on the right side of the motor, still easily within the driver's line of sight.

Some tractors have the remarkable convenience of an oil pressure adjustment near the pump, and therefore usually in the engine block. This allows a certain amount of control over the oil pressure with the insertion of shims (usually nothing more than coins or washers) to ensure that enough pressure is being generated by the pump to push oil up to the rocker arm assembly.

It seems kind of silly to explain what a DIP STICK is. The function of the oil system's dip stick is so simple, the word has become something of a common insult for someone who is equally simple! Yet, I have encountered people who either don't know what a dip stick is or don't bother checking it. I once stood in open-mouthed awe while an adult woman told me she changed the oil in her automobile regularly whenever the red oil pressure warning light on her dashboard came on. I made a mental note of the make and model of her car, and then vowed never to buy one like it from a used car dealer. In my mind, the oil reservoir dip stick is one of the most important—and neglected—gauges on an old tractor. Maybe it is so often forgotten because it's tucked down there alongside the motor: out of sight, out of mind.

Well, not for me! The dip stick tells you not only the level of your motor's oil reserve, but also its condition. You can tell from the oil on that stick how dirty the oil is. If it has a murky white color to it, then somewhere along the line water is getting into your oil—not a good thing. Not a good thing at all! Maintenance manuals for old tractors recommend checking the oil via the dip stick every time you're about to start it up. No one is that cautious on a modern vehicle, but frequent and regular checks are still a very good idea. On an old tractor, they are absolutely essential. (Note: If your tractor has a hydraulic system, there may also be a dip stick to check its oil.) Make sure you know which is which. My International 300 tractor has *three* dip sticks—one for the lubricating oil, a second for the hydraulic fluid, and a third for the transmission fluid. Don't be concerned if your tractor doesn't have a dip stick. Many older tractors simply have a drain cock at the optimum oil level on the side of the oil pan. The operator opens the cock and if no oil comes out, it needs more. It's a messy way of doing things, but it's simpler and just as effective.

Oil can be added to a tractor's reservoir in a variety of ways. On my Allis WCs, you can add oil through a special cap and breather near the magneto mount (thus also simultaneously giving the distributor shaft a bit of lubrication) or through the valve cover breather on top of the motor, often under a cap that protrudes through the hood of the tractor. A BREATHER is a protected opening where fumes from the oil system are vented.

The VISCOSITY of oil, or its resistance to flow—that is to say, its friction or, in a very general way, its thickness—is measured by a numbering system that often offers a split rating for its viscosity, cold and warm. Oil may simply be rated 10 weight, that would be a light oil with consistent viscosity, or maybe at 60 weight, which is much heavier but still consistent. Modern vehicles require a variable viscosity: an oil rated 10W40 is a light oil when it is cold and heavier when it is warm, thus letting a motor start more easily while still protecting it when it is hot. The number followed by a "W" indicates the oil's properties at low temperatures. The second number after the "W" speaks to higher temperatures. Modern oils may also contain a detergent, or cleaner. This can be a questionable virtue for old tractors. My first automobile was a 1939 clunker and I thought I'd do it a real favor by treating it to a dose of detergent oil. When the smoke cleared, the thing would barely run! Sometimes the only thing keeping a car's engine together is dirt!

The OIL FILTER may be the only filter on an old tractor, a sign of how important clean oil is to the operation of a machine under the kind of stresses a motor faces. The filter should be changed regularly, certainly every time the oil is changed, which should be often, in my opinion. On new tractors, the filter is a self-contained canister that screws or clamps into a special holder; to change it, you simply remove it and throw it away, and replace it with a clean new one. (Careful! Some filters come with a wooden stick in the middle to keep a spindle hole clear; it needs to be removed before installing the filter on its holder.) Other filters lack their own metal jacket and fit into a permanent metal canister that is part of the tractor's equipment. The canister is opened, the old, dirty filter removed and discarded, a new filter fitted onto the holder, and the canister holder is re-installed. If a rubber gasket is used to seal the canister, be sure your new filter includes a fresh one in the box before you throw away the old one!

Many old tractors use a BYPASS OIL FILTER SYSTEM. It would take a lot of energy from the motor and slow down the flow of oil as the filter clogs with contaminants, so the oil lines from the pump to other parts of the motor are sometimes split, with only *part* of the circulating oil going through the filter. Over time, of course, all of the oil in the motor passes through the filter. Yet, this is a compromise to keep the oil running and clean at the same time.

Though not really a part of the oil system, I'm going to stick another kind of crucial petroleum-based lubricant in here because oil changes and "lubes" are often thought of in the same breath. GREASE is an equally crucial element in servicing a tractor, and yet it is forgotten about as often as that blasted oil dip stick. No farm, shop, or machine shed is complete without a GREASE GUN, a small hand pump for forcing grease into GREASE ZERKS, small nipples that are placed around a tractor in spots where it is crucial to squeeze heavy grease to avoid wear. Zerks are found where there is a chance for metal to move on metal. A thin layer of grease keeps those pieces of metal from grinding each other away. The moral is, if you don't keep grease in those zerks, you're going to be replacing some expensive parts. To grease through a zerk, you simply push the business end of a grease gun onto the zerk—it will pop right on with a little pressure—and work the handle until a bit of grease can be seen oozing out of the joint you are lubricating.

There are also some joints where there are no zerks, but lubrication is clearly a good idea. On my Allis there are some GUIDES for the steering shaft, for example, where the solid steel steering shaft passes through a stationary tube to keep it aligned. There are no bearings to ease its rotation, just naked steel on naked steel. On my International 300, there are plenty of places on the rear implement hitch where there are no zerks but steel rolls in and against steel. I make a point of taking a little excess grease from a joint where it has oozed out, or simply squeeze a little from the grease gun onto a finger or rag to push manually onto and into those endangered places. That's probably the best thing and one of the easiest things I can do to keep my tractors running. All you have to do is look at a few old and neglected tractors to see the damage that kind of lack of care can cause. The mere thought of it almost brings tears to my eyes.

FUEL is stored in the FUEL TANK(S) of the tractor. If that seems all too obvious, it isn't. Like most things tractorial—I just made that word up—the situation is not quite as simple as it might seem. First of all, fuel is not fuel is not fuel. There are diesel and gasoline engines—okay, on tractors, *motors*—and they burn very different fuels, but that isn't the end of it. Old tractors were sometimes designed to burn KEROSENE, DISTILLATE, or TRACTOR FUEL, a low-grade—and therefore cheaper—gasoline. On tractors like my Allis WCs, the exhaust manifold could be turned over one way for the most efficient use of kerosene, or turned the other way for gasoline. Others like early Internationals had a MANIFOLD HEAT CONTROL that let the operator adjust the temperature of the incoming fuel-air mixture for easier combustion; it must be warmer for kerosene, distillate, and tractor fuel than it should be for gasoline.

It was not at all unusual for tractors back in the old days—like when I was a kid—to have two fuel tanks. One tank was for a half-gallon or so of gasoline for easy starting of the motor and a bit of warming up, and a larger tank was for less-expensive tractor fuel for long-term use. (A valve or set of valves permitted the operator to switch from gasoline to the cheaper fuel when the motor was warmed.)

A few tractors today run on propane with special regulators to deliver it to the cylinders, but this is not usually the stuff of old tractors and old-tractor nuts. I have picked up a few old tractors that were converted over to propane while they drove irrigation pumps. However, in those cases, my only concern was how to take all the adaptations off so I could return the machines to the fuels the tractor gods meant them to run on. Dave Mowitz reminds me that "propane or LP (liquefied petroleum) gas tractors were quite popular in the Midwest in the 1950s and 1960s, and they have become very collectible today. Deere propane or LP tractors bring double the price of conventional fuel machines." This brings up an issue that may seem contradictory for the new-tractor nut: propane-burning tractors are less common than conventional fuel tractors, but because they are rare, interesting, and more valuable, you are likely to find them as collectors' items. So you won't find as many of them in the average restorer's shop, but you'll find more than you might find elsewhere. Did I make that clear? Read it again.

Most old tractors released fuel from the tank(s) to the fuel lines, carburetor, and eventually the combustion cylinders by gravity: a fitting in the very bottom of the tank lets a small amount of fuel run down on its way to be burned by the motor. (Other and certainly later tractors may have automotive-style FUEL PUMPS to move fuel at a regulated pace to the carburetor and the motor, but that's the sort of thing you need to find out from operator's manuals and old-timers who are familiar with the machine you are interested in.) Usually the fuel ran out of the tank through a simple, fine-screen FUEL FILTER that caught any large debris that managed to get into the fuel or the tank, such as dirt, grain chaff, acorns, corn cobs, or tonic bottles. You'd be surprised at what you can find in the bottom of a tractor fuel tank! When I was first starting in this old tractor game, I had the incredibly good fortune of taking a restoration workshop with Oppie Gravert, an old, beloved, and now-gone master of the art. Along the way, he mentioned some of the things he'd found in the bottom of old tractor fuel tanks, including pieces of fuel gauges.

Now, I hadn't had a lot of experience at this point, but I'd never seen a fuel gauge on any Allis WCs, or for that matter on most of the other tractors I'd looked at. Of course, I was a novice, and I hadn't really *looked* for a gas gauge, but still . . . I raised my hand tentatively and when Oppie pointed to me, I said I'd like to know more about this gas gauge thing. I hadn't really seen many gas gauges even on newer models like my International 300, my Allis G, or my International Cub. There was a low chuckle from the older, more experienced shop veterans in attendance as, without a word, Oppie reached over and held up a stick. Okay, pieces of gas gauges—sticks—break off and fall into the tank. If a mechanic yells at you to bring him a gas gauge real quick, look for a clean stick.

Not far from the fuel tank, and often as not attached directly to its bottom at that hole from which the fuel runs, you'll find a SEDIMENT or SETTLING BOWL. This glass bowl is attached with a simple spring clamp to a fitting that houses the screen filter. Look into the glass bowl to see the fuel. You'll probably also see a little water, some gunk, a little grit, and maybe a stray ladybug or two if the screen filter has a hole in it. You will also find a small butterfly valve there that is used to shut off the fuel flow from the tank. To clean out the bowl or clean the screen filter, loosen the wire bail holding the glass bulb, take it off, clean off the screen, empty out whatever dirt or water you find in it, and clean it out.

Sometimes INLINE FUEL FILTERS have been added to the fuel line between the tank and the carburetor. An inline fuel filter is a small cylinder or bulb held onto the fuel line with small clamps. It ensures that clean fuel is delivered from the tank. While this kind of later addition is frowned on by restorers who insist on historical authenticity, they are mighty handy for those of us who enjoy our tractors as toys or use them as tools.

The FUEL LINE, usually a copper pipe or rubber tube, carries the fuel from the tank and its various filters and valves to the CARBURETOR. This is one of the most complicated parts of a tractor, as far as I'm concerned. I've never figured these things out. I do know two things about the carburetor: First, its function is to carefully mix a measured amount of fuel with the most effective amount of air and deliver the mixture to the intake manifold. Next it goes into the engine itself to be burned as a power source. Secondly, carburetor is spelled with one *A* and one *E*, not two *A*s. You want to be careful with this tidbit of information. Since most tractor mechanics I know spell the word "carbur*a*tor," you'll look like a real smarty-aleck if you make too much of a fuss about the proper spelling. Maybe the easiest thing to do would be to simply refer to it as the CARB. That'll do it.

The carb is going to be pretty close to the motor, about where the exhaust comes out, and maybe even attached to the exhaust and intake manifold. Inside the, uh, *carb*, things look pretty simple. There are some NEEDLE VALVES that allow for fine adjustment of the air and fuel, pretty much looking like what they sound like—pins with a thumb-knurl on one end, usually with a slot so you can also use a screwdriver, and a sharp point on the other. I do know that on most carbs there are two such valves; one you adjust for a smooth idle speed, the other for the best higher rpm performance. My impression is that there is no standard location for these adjustments. You'll have to check the manuals for your specific tractor or, better yet, ask an old-timer who is familiar with the tractor, or more likely the carburetor, since you may find any one of a wide variety of carburetor makes and models on various and assorted tractor makes. Ask your chosen old-timer to do an adjustment for you so you can see how it is done. Or, if you are like me, ask him or her to do an adjustment every few months because I never can figure out or remember which valve screw is for what or how exactly to do the whole carburetor adjustment finger dance.

Another troublesome item in the carb (a term that is often couched in a lot of cursing and snarling, so be prepared) is the FLOAT, a small metal bulb or set of bulbs that float in a small compartment that holds a pool of fuel inside the carb. As the float rises in the filled compartment, it closes another valve that restricts the amount of fuel coming in from the fuel line (and the fuel tank, of course). As the level of the fuel in the carb drops, and the motor burns and needs more fuel, the float falls and the valve opens. The opening valve lets more fuel in, almost exactly like the float in the tank of a toilet, if you are more familiar with household plumbing than carburetor construction.

The problem with the float—make that *problems*—is that it sometimes sticks inside the carb, and there's no easy way to get at it. This requires the most important of old tractor repair techniques: POUNDING THE CARBURETOR. For the pounding, preferably use a small piece of wood or small tool rather than a sledgehammer or monkey wrench. Light tapping will usually shake the float loose so it can go back to bobbing up and down inside the carb.

However, if the float has sprung a leak, it will sink to the bottom of the carb bowl like an invisible, tiny *Titanic* and lie there doing nothing at all. Then the motor won't work. Banging on the carburetor won't work either, no matter what size of tool you use. Then there is nothing to be done but dismantle the carb, and repair or replace the float. If you are around when someone is working on a carburetor and finds he has a carburetor float with a leak, you will learn a lot of new words.

Also associated with the carburetor is the CHOKE, a control used to adjust the air-fuel mixture when starting the tractor. On modern tractors and automobiles, the choke is automatic; you never have to concern yourself with it. But on old tractors there is a lever on the carburetor, sometimes manipulated by a wire or link to a lever or pull nearer the operator's seat, that operates this valve. After setting the choke and starting the motor, it usually doesn't take long before the operator can start to open the choke to resume normal operation of the carburetor. You'll learn very quickly how long to keep the choke closed on any particular tractor and how quickly to open it. It takes some finesse, and every motor is different.

The THROTTLE controls the speed of the motor by varying the amount of fuel going into the cylinders through the carburetor (and at the same time adjusts the motor's governor by means of an extension rod from the throttle). On automobiles, this is controlled by the operator with a foot pedal (or by an electronic setting called "cruise control"). On tractors, the throttle is usually a hand control, a lever or pull button that you can set so you can then spend the rest of the day taking care of everything else while the speed of the tractor remains constant.

The GOVERNOR adjusts the throttle and changes the engine's speed with information fed to it from the camshaft. When the motor comes under strain and slows down from the speed selected by the operator at the throttle, the governor lets the carburetor know and it sends more fuel into the cylinders.

From the carburetor, fuel is sucked up through the INTAKE MANIFOLD (often built into the same casting as the EXHAUST MANIFOLD on older tractors), pulled up through the intake valves, and into the cylinders where it is burned.

While it isn't strictly a part of the fuel system, I am going to talk briefly about the AIR FILTER here because it is an integral part of the carburetion process, which *is* a part of the fuel system. Modern cars have air cleaners even though the air along highways is fairly clean. Yet think about the huge amounts of air a modern engine pulls in, and then imagine how much dirt and dust go into it when you are pounding along a gravel road in the country!

Well, a tractor isn't purring along a nice paved highway, sucking relatively clean air into the carburetor. Nope, our sweethearts are always out there in the dirt, dust, bugs, sand, grit, water, smoke, chaff and who knows what all. If you're sucking all that junk into the carburetor to mix with the fuel before sending it to the motor, well, you can imagine. It wouldn't take long for the carb to fill up with muck and goo, and for the parts in the engine to be completely worn by all the garbage sucked through them. So, the air being brought into that motor has to be as clean as you can make it.

Most tractor air cleaners are basic, but effective. Air is pulled in through an inverted intake, so nothing falls in from above and larger pieces simply fall away before being sucked in. Then there is a coarse screen or baffle, a piece of steel with holes in it to keep out the big stuff. Then a container filled with steel-wool-like metal shavings filters out smaller but still substantial hunks of dirt and grit. Finally, the air is pulled through a cup of light oil in the bottom of the filter in which the really fine dirt and dust is captured. This cup is always easily accessible and removable, so the filthy oil can be dumped and the new oil can be poured in. This should be done frequently, not just to protect the motor, but also to protect the air cleaner because water often accumulates in the bottom of the cup and can rust through it if left in there long. If you're helping out a tractor person in a shop and you want to do something useful, ask if you can change the oil in the air filter. He'll figure you can't do much damage there, so what the heck? He'll be impressed that you know there's oil in the base of that oil cleaner too. Unless, of course, you mistake the oil filter for the air filter and dump a couple quarts of dirty oil on the shop floor when you screw it off. Hmmm . . . maybe you better not volunteer for anything quite yet.

On a modern working tractor, you just have to have hydraulics—that's all there is to it. My International 300 is the machine I use around here for hauling things in the bucket, plowing snow, plowing fields, pulling trailers, digging postholes, and mowing. And believe me, if it weren't for the HYDRAULICS, my life would be one misery after another. Hydraulics are what lift and move everything that attaches to the tractor, not to mention powering the power brakes and steering. The only *old* tractor I have with a hydraulic setup is a 1950 Allis WD; the hydraulics raise and lower the blade that is permanently mounted on the back end. I once tried to rebuild a WD, but stopped at the hydraulic system. I just don't get it. The pumps and valves are beyond me. But maybe I can give you at least some idea of what a hydraulic system is in case you run into one.

The hydraulic oil system is a lot like the lubricating oil system we discussed above. There is a RESERVOIR in which a supply of oil is kept, but in this case it is HYDRAULIC FLUID, oil specifically formulated for the high heat and high compression of hydraulic work. A HYDRAULIC PUMP pulls oil from the reservoir and forces it past HYDRAULIC VALVES that let you determine by means of hand levers which hoses the fluid is going to move along and in which direction. The pump is a good deal stronger than the one that moves lubricating oil around your tractor's motor, but the force of the hydraulic fluid is multiplied substantially by inserting it into large cylinders, or RAMS, through small apertures. It turns out that if you force liquid into a large cylinder through a small hole, it goes in pretty easy, slowly but easily. Of course, this also means that the large cylinder moves rather slowly too, but with much greater force than you might expect. You throw a lever, and oil from the ferociously powerful pump goes through a surprisingly small—but very strong—hose into a larger cylinder, and that cylinder moves with a greater force than you can imagine, lifting enormous weights and applying ferocious force. That's precisely what you want for lifting things like front-end buckets full of sand and dirt, or hoisting a plow or cultivator out of the ground.

As I mentioned earlier, there should also be a dip stick for the hydraulics reservoir. If your tractor has hydraulics but you don't see a dip stick, look for a drain cock on the reservoir. You want to be sure to check the fluid level often, not only to make sure you have plenty of fluid in the system, but that it is clean and doesn't have that milky white cast to it that tells you there is water in the system. If that water freezes up in the valves or filters in your hydraulics system, you have real trouble. And it's even worse if your tractor is like my International where the hydraulics reservoir and pump also serve the power steering and brakes, and what's more, is at the same time providing the fluid in the transmission! That hydraulic fluid serves a lot of purposes and you don't want to sell short the importance of keeping track of its condition when it comes to maintenance and keeping your tractor running smoothly.

Wifey Linda insists that I have omitted the two most familiar, usual, and apparently essential fluids associated with old tractors and certainly with any mechanic intending to work with them: blood and sweat. I'd love to argue with her about that, but cannot for the life of me think of a suitable response. I know what fluids are most common when I spend time in the shop. Yep, she's right: blood and sweat. And an occasional cold beer.

CHAPTER 5

ELECTRICAL
(VIS-À-VIS OLD TRACTORS)

I I'm not even sure I believe in electricity. I know it's there, but, really, where is it? You can't see it. Can we really accept something we can't see as real? If my knowledge of mechanics is recent and fundamental, my understanding of electricity is nonexistent and unlikely. But tractors—all of them—do have an electrical system, even if it's primitive and simple, so I am going to do the best I can to give you some idea of the electrical parts of an old tractor you are likely to encounter as a newcomer. (Please note here and in the title of this chapter that I cover my rear by making it clear that not only is my knowledge of electricity primitive, but what I do have pertains only to *old* tractors!) Maybe my innocence is an advantage here again because I'm sure not going to overwhelm or intimidate you with my incredible knowledge of such things!

I suspect that that is, in fact, one reason I love working with old tractors: There's a lot less not to understand, especially when it comes to electricity. On my special favorite, the Allis-Chalmers WC tractor, there are exactly four electrical wires, one to each of the four spark plugs. That much I understand.

Even faced with something as obvious and uncomplicated as that, it's where my grasp of the WC's electrical system ends. And I'm not alone. You can *see* pistons, gears, levers, and shafts, but you can't *see* electricity. It's mysterious stuff, and I'm not the only one who is baffled by it. I know a lot of people who know a lot about tractor mechanics. But there are two things that will make them shake their heads in confusion and defeat: carburetors and magnetos.

I invite you to try a little test to demonstrate my point here. Go to someone you respect when it comes to mechanical knowledge and ask him or her, "How does a magneto work?" I think you will find the reaction you get enlightening. People who understand magnetos, condensers, distributors, and points—electricity in general—are held in an esteem usually reserved for mystic wizards, by even the very best of mechanics. Electricity is a specialty, and a rare one at that.

That goes triple for those who understand the MAGNETO. It doesn't help that magnetos are many generations back in the history of tractors; before alternators, before generators, there were magnetos. I vaguely understand that an electrical current is generated when a coil is passed through a magnetic field. I know that there is a permanent magnet in a tractor's magneto, and a coil on a rotor that turns within and thus passes through that magnet's field. That movement generates the electrical current that energizes the mag's coil, which provides the spark that ignites the fuel and forces the piston to turn the crankshaft, and so on.

I'm already trying to explain things way beyond me, as my buddy Dick pointed out to me when he read this part of the text. But I will try nonetheless to give you at least a start on the electrics of an old tractor. A tractor has either a magneto or a generator, each with a coil somewhere in it or connected to it, and a component function to distribute the pulses of electrical energy along wires to the spark plugs to ignite the fuel in the cylinders. I think. I get tired just thinking about it.

Of course, the electricity doesn't run through the spark plug wires on a constant basis. It needs to reach the plugs at just the right time, and that's really what a lot of a tractor's electrical system is about—sending a jolt of juice along to those plugs at just the right time and in just the right order. The DISTRIBUTOR does that: *distributes* the electricity. A small rotor inside the distributor case swings an arm round a series of POINTS, contacts spaced around the inside of the case. As the arm swings around inside the case and makes contact with the points, a brief jolt of electricity is sent from the source—the coil—and down the wire attached to the spark plug. Inside the distributor, you will find a CONDENSOR (a term disputed by modern fancy-dansies who insist that it's actually a CAPACITOR), a small canister or wrapped bundle that is like a small storage battery; it accumulates and stores electricity for a moment in the electrical cycling and then releases it to the plugs as a more powerful and timed jolt.

The TIMING of a tractor is the adjustment that makes sure the current goes through the plug and provides the spark at just the right moment—when the piston is at the TOP DEAD CENTER (also known as TDC) of that cylinder in the compression part of its cycle.

A tractor's FIRING ORDER is the sequence in which that happens; cylinders in a tractor motor don't always fire and provide their power in regular order, right on down the engine from the first cylinder to the second and then the third and fourth, fifth, and sixth or whatever. (I joke with my in-laws that the reason they prefer two-cylinder tractors is that they can then remember the firing order! 1-2-1-2-1-2. Or is it 2-1-2-1-2-1?) On my Allis WCs, the firing order is 1-2-4-3. I have no idea why.

Brace yourself here for a substantial but important aside in our discussion about the electrics of old tractors!

Several times in this book I have recommended that when you have specific questions about tractor problems, you should consider going to one of the several, useful chat sites dealing with tractors on the web. Well, as I wrote the last sentence of the previous paragraph, I did exactly that. I went to the Antique Tractor Internet Service (ATIS) tractor chat site and asked if anyone could give me a short and simple explanation for why firing orders aren't straightforward 1-2-3-4. And man, did I ever get some interesting information! Over the next couple days after I posted my query, I received more than 70 helpful, humorous, and, yes, no kidding, fascinating responses. (And one poster reassured me that the phrase should really be "firing *dis*order!")

Perhaps the shortest and simplest explanation I got for why cylinders are fired in various orders was "BALANCE!" And I suspect that is precisely it. Another poster explained that every time a piston fires and presses its rod against that crankshaft with ferocious force, the engine wants to lurch to one side. In fact, engine blocks actually *flex* microscopically with the violence of those firings. If a set of harmonic firings were set up, the engine would twist itself from its mounts and shake itself apart. Engineers who know about such things therefore set up an engine—or motor, as the case may be—so that insofar as possible, the firing pistons offset each other in their gigantic forces. They are not putting too much pressure on any one section of the crankshaft, not working against each other, and not working destructively together. It's some kind of *balancing* act going on in there!

Roughly that same kind of balancing act goes on at a site like ATIS You ask a question and you get information, ranging from too simple to be of much use to stuff so complicated I can't possibly understand it. And very quickly the "thread," the line of conversation at the chat site, moves on well beyond the question to discussions about radial airplane engines, crankshafts operating in one plane (not an airplane, I presume), motor-cycle engines, and even racing engines. (I was amazed to learn some mechanics set a four-cylinder engine so that two cylinders fire at the same time, thus providing more "bite" on the track!).

And trivia. Earlier in this discussion, for example, I noted that the distributor makes sure an impulse of electricity is sent along the line only at the top of the compression stroke. Well, it turns out that's not exactly true. In some engines, the impulses are sent far more often, and simply go to waste. It was easier to do it that way, apparently, than to go through the trouble of figuring out a way to cut some impulses off. Who would have guessed?

My favorite response to my query came from Charlie Hill at the ATIS site. Charlie, an ATIS regular, gave me a totally new perspective on the firing order of my Allis WCs. Charlie said that the engine's firing order is the engineer's way of ensuring engine "balance." Then he said something that really stunned me because it speaks to my own perspective, or lack thereof. He said, "[The firing order] 1-2-4-3 seems awkward when you read it that way but it is actually firing every other cylinder in order. If you start with 2 instead of 1, it would be 2-4-3-1. When you think about it, that is in order. On your Allis engine . . . the crank is all in one plane. I mean, two crank lobes are up and two are down."

Wow! Charlie is precisely right! Just starting that sequence with the second number *two* instead of my arithmetic-centric, culturally demanded *one*, does make the sequence logical! Every other cylinder! 2-4-3-1! That revelation really makes me wonder how many other things that I am stumped by could be simplified and explained with just one simple shift and starting somewhere other than what seems most logical in the customary way of thinking!

See? Working on an old tractor in your shop isn't just tinkering. It's an exercise in philosophy and perspective, logic and culture. For me, finding out about something like this is a matter of renewed vitality: I'm 67 years old at this writing, and still learning.

Somewhere along the line of an old tractor's electrical system, you may also find a COIL, a canister about the size of a soup can that is usually mounted close to the distributor. Wires run to and from the coil, which amplifies the power in such a way (like a transformer, in case you understand that technology) that it goes from being a fairly mild current to something that will knock your socks off if you make the mistake of touching the wrong things at the wrong moment and become yourself a part of that tractor's electrical circuits. My old and very much mourned friend Don Hochstetler was once making some adjustments on a running tractor of mine on the main street of my little town and I was looking on, trying to learn whatever I could from him. All at once, he jumped back. I asked him, "Did you get a shock?" Without a moment of hesitation, Don said, "Nope. I was too fast for it."

A SOLENOID (SWITCH or CELL) is a wire coil with a sliding rod inside the coil. When electricity is run through the coil, the rod moves in or out; thus, a solenoid is an electrically activated switch. You often find one on older tractors, mounted on or near and working with the starting motor. That's because a solenoid is used to engage the gear of the starting motor with the flywheel. Once engaged, the solenoid holds the gear in place while power is sent on to the motor itself to turn that flywheel. Once the flywheel is flying, the solenoid retreats and moves the gear out of the way.

I mentioned SPARK PLUGS earlier in these pages, but since they are a part of the tractor's electrical system, I'll discuss them in more detail here. Of course, the plugs provide the little spark that ignites the fuel in the cylinders. I don't think I mentioned, however, that a crucial and common consideration in spark plugs is the **GAP**. The spark leaps across two terminals on the end of the plug that is inside the motor, and the distance between those two terminals—the gap—works best when it is juuuuust right. Adjustment of the gap is a fairly simple process: a feeler gauge, plug gauge, or gapper of the appropriate distance, indicated on the gauge in thousandths of an inch, is inserted between the two terminals on the plug. The long arm of the plug is then gently pressed or tapped until the fit of the gauge between the terminals is firm, but not tight. The gauge is usually a feeler gauge—a thin leaf of metal of the appropriate thickness—or a wire gauge with a series of loops or pegs of wire of the appropriate thickness. The operator's manual for your tractor will tell you what the gap on your spark plugs should be.

I think I have just about covered all the components of the most basic antique tractor electrical systems. As we move further down the historical line, tractors grow ever more complicated in every dimension, including electrical. As you look at tractors ever later in agricultural history, you will run into some of the following terms and items. It would be a real stretch to call the four spark plug wires of my Allis-Chalmers WC a **WIRING HARNESS**, but take just one step down history's path to the WD, the next Allis-Chalmers model in line, and you will find that word in the parts list. A wiring harness is a bundled set of wires with most of the wires, or probably darn near *all* the wires, for the entire tractor. You buy a wiring harness as one unit, string it through the requisite holders and clips, and attach the ends where indicated, and *voila*! Your tractor is rewired!

Even with antique tractors, you may find a GENERATOR providing the electrical power instead of a magneto. A generator looks like an electric motor, and kind of is, but the opposite. Instead of using electricity to drive a rotor, as is the case for the motor in a household fan, the rotor of a generator is usually turned by a FAN BELT running from the front of the crankshaft (which may also be running the water pump along the way), and the turning rotor of the generator *generates* electricity. The principal of the generator is the same as the magneto: spin a coil through a magnetic field.

Since you are now making more electricity than you need with this newfangled generator device, you can store some of it in a STORAGE BATTERY, a box containing plates and BATTERY ACID (also called BATTERY FLUID) that actually stores up electricity for later use. (Battery acid is really dangerous stuff. Be careful with it, not only avoid getting it on your skin or in your eyes, but on anything else. This stuff will eat a hole in concrete!) Batteries have POSITIVE and NEGATIVE TERMINALS. Don't mix up those two unless you really want to see sparks fly and wires burn!

Electricity flows in a loop and needs to have a closed CIRCUIT to flow. That's why everything that uses electricity has at least two wires running to it (and maybe a third GROUND). One of the terminals on the battery is the ground, and it is simply attached to the tractor's frame. Then everything that needs to complete the circuit by having a ground is simply attached to the grounded frame. The ground can be either positive or negative—again, we are going beyond the scope of my knowledge of such things. You better check with your tractor's manual or a friendly old-tractor nut who knows about machines like yours.

Batteries come in a lot of different sizes, as you've probably discovered when you got a new toy for Christmas. The instructions say you need to put a 9-volt battery in it. Of course, all you have are AAA batteries. You also have some AAs and a couple of As. And a B. And two microbatteries. It always works that way. What's more important, batteries also contain different voltages—that is, amounts of electricity. Well, on an old tractor, you are generally going to find 6-volt batteries. You probably won't find them anywhere else. Most modern vehicles like your car use 12-volt batteries. And occasionally you'll run into an 8-volt battery. While you generally don't want to mix these things up, don't be surprised to find a mechanic with some experience using a 12-volt battery or 12-volt portable battery unit to start a tractor that normally requires a 6-volt battery. Brief use of a 12-volt power source on a 6-volt system usually won't cause any problems, and it provides a hotter spark with a more certain motor start. Don't keep that 12-volt power hooked up to those 6-volt terminals very long or things will start to smoke, gauges will be ruined, and fuses will blow!

My tractor buddy Dick suggests that I should perhaps add here that along the line some nut is going to tell you that you will get much better performance and quicker starts if you put an 8-volt battery in a 6-volt system. Bad idea! There's no safe way to charge the battery in this kind of setup because, according to Dick, "All nonindustrial chargers handle only 6 or 12 volts. I spoke with a tech at Exide once about this and he said the 8-volt batteries are designed for industrial applications and should never be used elsewhere." That sounds about right to me. But what do I know?

FUSES are replaceable items. On old tractors, they are usually little glass tubes with metal ends enclosing a strip of soft metal that is calibrated to melt away when too much power goes through it, and it gets too hot. A fuse is one tractor part that is designed to fail, and you want it to fail when its time comes up; it breaks the faulty circuit before anything else burns up, like the starting motor, gauges, or anything else electrical on your machine. Even many antique tractors have a fuse somewhere on them, usually behind a control panel where you find the gauges and switches if there are any. When your electrical system won't cooperate, the fuse is a good place to start looking for the problem.

An enormous advantage in the development of the generator and storage battery and inclusion of them on tractors was the wonderful result that one no longer needed to crank the motor over by hand to start it. And then go to the hospital to have broken wrists, arms, jaws, and noses set. I have never really minded the brief but strenuous effort of turning a tractor crank because I figure not having a starting motor means there's one more thing I don't have to worry about going on the fritz on a motor vehicle. (You can tell I tend to be somewhat cynical about such things.) But I am troubled by the inherent dangers of a hand crank.

I wasn't at all worried about such things until one day in town I cranked over my WC, but didn't hear the absolutely essential sound of the impulse pawl clicking and thereby indicating that the cranking operation was going along nicely and safely. The crank snapped back, hitting me smartly between my right wrist and elbow. It hurt to beat billy-hell, but what really worried me was the enormous lump, about the size of a grapefruit, that almost immediately sprang up where the crank handle had hit me. My arm wasn't broken (I guess—I never went to the hospital or doctor to have it checked of course, being a man and all), but I sure have approached tractor cranks with more respect since that moment.

If your tractor has a STARTING MOTOR, you can relax. You won't face that danger of hand cranking your tractor. A tractor's starting motor might be found in a number of places around the motor itself: the front, the rear, or off to one side. You'll just have to check with someone who knows or consult a manual for your machine. On my Allis WD, the starting motor is plain as can be, right by the operator's feet, and geared to turn over the flywheel to start the motor. I like this arrangement because it is easy for a tyromechanic like me to remove it, look at it, see how it works, or why it doesn't, and then replace it.

While modern automobiles always have a key to start them with, on old tractors you are more likely to find a switch that is flipped up or down, and then something you push or pull to start the motor. On my old International 300, I push a button on the control panel to start the motor; on my Allis WD, I pull a small wire loop under the steering wheel; on my G, one starts the motor by pulling a wire connector that comes up through a hole in the right fender. I'm not kidding—the starter pull control comes up through a hole in the right fender! On my brand-spanking-new, sparkly bright AGCO ST-55 tractor, I turn the ignition switch on the panel counterclockwise until the glow plug light comes on (it's a diesel), then I turn it to the right, tuning in an instant musical roar of an engine perfectly tuned and eager to do my every bidding. Do I love my new tractor? Like a new puppy, I love my new tractor!

LIGHTS are probably self-explanatory. Some older tractors have lights, some don't. Few are sealed beams like modern ones—that is, single units that simply plug in rather than parts one dismantles and inserts an incandescent bulb. However, I should perhaps note that a tractor's light switch often is also a control for the amount of power the generator is asked to produce and send through the battery. A tractor switch may have two settings, one for simple daylight operation and a second with higher production of power for fast recharge and operation of additional electrical devices like lights.

If your tractor has a control panel, probably the one gauge you will find there—if there is only one—will be an AMMETER, a device that measures the amount of electricity being produced by the generator. (And if your tractors are anything like mine, the ammeter will no longer be working.) You are in fact more likely to find an ammeter on your tractor than a gas gauge! On a lot of automobiles these days there is only a red light that comes on when your electrical power system fails and it's too late to do anything. You won't find that on an old tractor.

Another gauge that you might find on a tractor that you may not find on an automobile's control panel is a TACHOMETER (or TACH), showing you the RPM (REVOLUTIONS PER MINUTE) of your crankshaft, that is, the engine speed. You need to know that because a lot of agricultural equipment requires fairly specific rpm to operate at its maximum efficiency. In fact, on my International 300 the only thing close to a speedometer is a set of parameters behind the tach needle that tells me roughly how fast I might be moving in the various gears at various rpm's! What a tractor is making by way of miles per hour, it seems, is not as important as the revolutions per minute its crankshaft or PTO are turning.

Associated with a tach, you may find a counter indicating the number of hours the tractor has been operating. Again, I didn't know what the heck you call this thing. It looks like an automobile's odometer, which is, believe it or not, what you call that thing that measures mileage, but the counter on my tractor measures time. Again I went to the ATIS site and asked if anyone there could help me put a name on this device. Within moments, Charlie Hill told me that if it mechanically measures rotational speed (probably, he says, of the PTO) then it is a kind of tach. If it is electric, then it is a clock, and hence, an hour meter. Mike Sloane offers that he has heard it referred to as a "proof," although he doesn't know what it proves. Isn't it amazing what these guys know?

The next day the ATIS discussion about this device continued. John Cable wrote that in the navy, a gauge like this was called an Op Hour Meter (for operational hours). Stuart Harner reported that in his experience it is called a Hobbs meter, after the manufacturer, although he had also heard "proof meter" and "hour meter," while the reading is referred to as "tach time." R. Mull noted that Ford called it a "proof meter."

The bottom line is, if you have a question about even the most obscure tractor issues, a web tractor chat room is the place to go ask it.

Unless one of your best friends happens to be The Ulti-Magni-Tractor Techie, Dave Mowitz at *Successful Farming*. I get to go directly to him and so I did on this poser. He says, "The official industry term for this is hour meter. All other terms, particularly 'proof,' are homespun terms.

Today's hour meters and tachs are electric. However, all hour meters on tractors prior to the mid-1980s were mechanical, not electrical, and worked off the same mechanical shaft that turned the tach." (I have to note, without contradicting Dave, that from tyros to pros we do all have to deal with those "homespun" terms, even more than we do the "official industry" nomenclature.)

Unless you intend to become an expert yourself, or are perhaps coming to the world of tractor restoration as an expert already, resources like the ATIS site are precisely the kind of thing you are going to have to draw on. I suspect that an expert in antique tractor electrical systems is not likely to be a hydraulics expert. A clutch specialist may not know diddly about valves. But man, when you put together the entire resources of all the people who regularly check in at and post on the ATIS website—or the Yesterday's Tractors site, or Ageless Iron—you have a range of top-notch experts. These folks know far more than any one human being will ever know on his own. They comprise a team of consultants all working for nothing and what's really great is that they do it cheerfully. If you are going to get into working on old tractors, don't for an instant underestimate the circle of friends you will find in the world of old tractors, even if you never meet a single one of them in person.

CHAPTER 6

STEERING AND BRAKES

This far along in a protracted exploration of the various parts of an old tractor, we are bound to be having some overlap, and so we have. I have already talked about the tractor's front pedestal without discussing at that point the steering mechanisms, but that's what that pedestal is for, in large part. So please forgive me and understand that as we go *back* to revisit some of these parts and places.

Different tractors use different systems to transmit the turning of the STEERING WHEEL in the operator's hands and down to the front wheels. Sometimes the STEERING SHAFT runs from the steering wheel atop the steering wheel column and over the top of the motor, as it does in Linda's John Deere B. Sometimes it is offset to run alongside the motor, as it is with my Allis WCs. The steering shaft runs through a series of GUIDES, pieces of steel tubing mounted on or in the frame that hold the shaft and give it support. The shaft then goes into the front pedestal, where it is geared to transfer the horizontal rotation of the steering wheel vertically down to the front wheels. Along the way, there may be a UNIVERSAL JOINT in the steering shaft, which is a flexible knuckle that allows bending and wiggling of the shaft without compromising its strength.

Some tractors, usually rare, and therefore all the more desirable by collectors, had only one front wheel and tire, mounted in a fork arrangement, but most tractors had two. (If and when you see an old tractor with a single front wheel—they use one up at our Co-op here in town—be sure to stop or at least slow down and yell, "Hey Mister! You lost one of your front wheels!" They expect it.)

And most old tractors have what is called a TRICYCLE MOUNT, or NARROW FRONT END (often abbreviated in sale bills, advertisements, published descriptions, and such as NF), with the front wheels much closer together than the back wheels. This arrangement is not quite as safe and stable as a WIDE FRONT (WF), where the front wheels are spread as wide or about as wide as the back, but it had advantages for field work where the front wheels could be focused into a single furrow in the field. (Wide front ends usually are adjustable so that the wheels could be moved in and out to accommodate the spacing of furrows for plows, planters, cultivators, and other field equipment.) Narrow-front tractors trade a certain amount of stability for the ability to turn more sharply.

I don't want to get too fussy here, but sometimes in manuals or tech guides you will find that words we use fairly casually in daily life are used in much more specific ways elsewhere. For example, what is an AXLE? Mmmm . . . I guess the heavy rod the wheels are mounted on and rotate around, right? Well, yes and no. In technical manuals, you are likely to find that mechanics think of axles as the main crossmembers of a vehicle's suspension, and on the axle there are SPINDLES, on which the wheels rotate. You may also find that in the little guy's shop, language is more as described by the Queen of Hearts in *Alice in Wonderland*, meaning exactly what we want it to mean. So you'll have to get used to aluminum being referred to as "alumiam," and clutches being called "clunches." At this stage of your education, I don't recommend that you make the mistake of trying to correct the Tractor University professors.

A tractor's BRAKES may be operated by a foot pedal, or more likely two foot pedals, or a hand lever, or two hand levers. BRAKE PADS, SHOES, or BANDS are pressed against a BRAKE DISC or BRAKE DRUM (on either the inside or the outside, depending on the tractor).

While modern brakes are hydraulic systems with a main cylinder, brake lines, and cylinders at each braking wheel, antique tractor brakes are usually mechanical and you can easily follow the cables, rods, pedals, and levers to see how the mechanics of a braking system work. That also makes repair work a lot easier for those of us who are not professionals.

Perhaps most interesting and surprising to a newcomer to old tractors is the notion of separate brakes for the left and right rear wheels. (The front wheels of a tractor are virtually never braked.) A novice's first impression is, "How dumb! When you apply the right brake pedal or lever, the tractor pulls hard over to that side!" Exactly! That's the idea. A tractor is a working tool and sometimes we place much more severe demands on it than we might have on an automobile. What's more, a tractor is a slower vehicle than an automobile, so we can afford to ask more dramatic movements from it.

So there are times, maybe at the end of a field as you approach the fence or ditch, when you need to turn the tractor, and you need to turn it hard and fast. If you merely turn the steering wheel, you not only get a slow reaction turn, because there is likely to be a lot of weight on the rear and drive wheels of the tractor and very little on the front, your front wheels may actually want to "push," or skid, instead of turn. This situation is amplified by the weight of the implement you are pulling, if you are pulling an implement. Well, if you are turning that wheel to the left and you simultaneously press the left brake pedal or pull back on the left brake lever, you are going to turn left, and I mean *right now*! It is possible on many tractors to make a hard, fast turn in either direction without the rear wheel on that side moving at all except to swivel on itself, the front wheels and one rear wheel of the tractor describing a perfect circle with the other rear wheel serving as the exact center. Don't try this with any kind of speed; believe me, even at slow speeds you want to make sure you are securely seated and hanging on tight!

At this very moment, as I write this, my overalls are drying out from an hour of clearing 2 feet of snow from our drive. The hydraulics on the

International are frozen up, so I had to revert to the old faithful Allis WD. It isn't easy to deal with the WD's hydraulics. They're not live hydraulics and it's a fairly primitive setup, so adjustments are not nearly as fine as on the International. The WD's tires are old and tired, so I don't get a lot of traction with that tractor. It doesn't have a bucket that would allow me to lift the snow and throw it over the bushes somewhere or into the ditch. The worst problem with using the WD in snow is that the front end is so light and the tires are so worn, that it is virtually impossible to turn this thing on the snow. It just keeps sliding straight ahead no matter how hard I turn the steering wheel or yell at it "Gee! Haw! Gee! Damn it, turn, you no good @#$%&$#@, turn!"

So imagine trying to maneuver a tractor with a blade on the back with no steering at the wheel. What's to do? Well, you have to steer it with your feet, that's what. I turn the wheel for what good it does, but most of the work of turning is done by pushing the right and left brakes. Without that alternative, it would be the ancient theory of snow removal, "God put it there, let God take it away." Operating a tractor in this manner is a wild dance—spinning the steering wheel, stomping on a left pedal and then the right—it helps to know how to do the polka.

Almost all tractors also have a BRAKE SET, LOCK, or LATCH, a device (lever, pedal, knob) that can be engaged to lock the brakes. This control is very useful when operating stationary equipment like a mill or buzz saw when you want to make sure that tractor isn't going to move once you have it set where you want it. Make sure you release that brake lock before you try to get the tractor moving ahead again!

CHAPTER 7

SMALL PARTS

I wrote earlier in these pages that there were places where I simply had to draw the line, that there were going to be things I simply could not include because I can't include everything, not to mention that as a beginner you don't need to know everything. This is definitely one of those places. I have completely dismantled—completely—several tractors, right down to nuts, bolts, washers, pins, gaskets, doodads, and thingamabobs. I like to think that there are very few parts, no matter how small, of my own particular favorite tractor, the Allis-Chalmers WC, that I couldn't identify.

I know for a fact that I couldn't sit down and list them all. I mean, think about it. Can you imagine how many little bitty parts there are in a tractor? Each and every part has a name: a Woodruff key, a straight key, a hairpin clip, a C-clip, a keeper, a pilot bearing, a cone bearing, blah blah blah blah

blah blah blah . . . I have to remind you and myself of what I have in mind for this book: To help you understand someone else who knows all this stuff. I want to let you be a part of the fun, and to keep you from making a total fool of yourself when your friend sends you over to his tool bench to get him a cotter pin and you bring him a bowling pin instead. He'll be talking about you up at the Co-op for years to come!

Kinda like my old man the time I wanted to fix an old chair I was particularly fond of. Wanting to be helpful, he said, "Okay, Rog, here's what you do. Go down to my shop and get a drill and a little bit." I popped up and asked, "Uh, a little bit of what?" He looked at me a minute and went back to reading his paper. You don't want that to happen to you.

You won't believe how many kinds of nuts and bolts there are. You'd think that nothing could be simpler than a bolt and a nut. In the beginning, I suppose that was true, but things sure have gotten complicated over the years. Fortunately for us old tractor enthusiasts, traveling back in time also takes us back in complications, so there are not quite as many things to worry about with old tractors as the mechanic who works on modern machinery is likely to encounter. But still, we have some sorting to do here. If you want to explore more extensively the wide and wonderful world of fasteners, I highly recommend *Nuts, Bolts, Fasteners, and Plumbing Handbook* by Carroll Smith. (MBI Publishing, same good guys who published the book you have in your hands!) Smith tells you astonishing things about fasteners, no kidding, and you will be amazed at how complex something as simple as a nut and bolt can be. I can imagine you snorting at the suggestion that something like a bolt can actually be interesting, but I'm serious about this one. Even if you have never given 10 seconds of thought to a bolt before, I'm betting that once you start leafing through this book, you are going to be shaking your head in amazement before long.

Another way to learn about hardware and parts is to get to know the folks at your local Fastenal, Centaur Fasteners, or similar store—even Home Depot, Ace Hardware, or Menards. They can help you put together a starter package of commonly used fasteners and they'll be your best source for hard-to-find hardware in the future. Just walk the aisles, read labels, look at stuff. You'll be amazed not only at the variety of things you see, but also how truly interesting this stuff can be.

For sure, get to know the people at the closest outlet for the kinds of tractor in which you have an interest. Often they too love old tractors and have an interest in them and have ancient parts stored away in the parts department. Moreover, you will find, if your experience is like mine, that dealers in tractor parts are not at all like people behind the counters of modern auto parts outlets. Tractor people tend to be more willing to help you, to spend time educating you, to know what they are talking about, and to be willing to go to some effort to help you find what you need, even for a tractor that they haven't sold for 50 years or more.

As for actual tractor parts, nothing beats dismantling a tractor. You will quickly find that rebuilding an antique tractor often means buying more than *one* tractor. Yes, there is the machine you are rebuilding, repairing, or restoring, but behind almost every tractor mechanic's shop you will also find a PARTER, or PARTS TRACTOR, another derelict that is being cannibalized for parts. In my own case, there is no BONEYARD, or tractor salvage yard within 50 miles. I go to Stromp's Dump, the boneyard of my good friend Jim Stromp, that is about 60 miles from here about once a year, but it's just not that easy to make a parts run that is over an hour in each direction on a regular basis.

There is a really good Allis dealership just a half hour from here, and they are very helpful with new parts. The first time I went there, I went with a coffee can of parts I wanted to replace and came home with that coffee can half-full of parts that cost me nearly a hundred dollars. I figured out that I simply couldn't afford to buy new parts on a regular basis either. After all, at that time I was buying junked Allis-Chalmers WC tractors at IRON PRICE, roughly what the tractor would bring at a junkyard for the value of the iron in it.

I called Linda out to the shop yard because I knew that explaining what was about to happen in advance would be the diplomatic thing to do. It was clear to me that I was going to be buying, hauling, and lining up along our windbreak some old salvage tractors for parters. I showed her the can of new parts and the bill; then I showed her a wrecked WC I had recently hauled in and showed her the check stub for it. Both were for about the same amount of money. She understood that kind of logic, and I started buying up and hauling in junked tractors.

From that experience I also realized several things: First, it wasn't a good idea to take the head off of a parter and then just let it sit out there in the rain and wind for a couple more years. Second, some of the most fun I had with tractors was taking them apart. Perhaps most importantly, I never learned more than I did when I was dismantling a tractor. When the time finally came when I needed a part, I wasn't going to be very happy about having to crawl around under a wreck in the snow or heat and take that part off of a wreck. So I did one of the smartest things I have done in my short career in tractor mechanicking: I picked a wreck that I knew I wouldn't be rebuilding and I totally dismantled it. I cleaned the parts as I progressed, labeled them, packed them in plastic bags, put them in cans and boxes, and set them on sturdy shelves in what I came to call the parts bay of my tractor shed.

It was such fun that I did the same with a couple of other tractors. I not only had great fun and took enormous satisfaction from doing that, but I was also pretty darn proud of myself the first time I needed a part and strolled into my parts bay. I took a nice, clean, refurbished part off the shelf without having to face the Nebraska weather out by the windbreak.

The moral of this story is: When you get serious about tractors, and maybe come to a decision on one particular make and model that you want to work with, do consider acquiring a second (even a third or fourth) example of that same machine for parts. A parter can be in pretty terrible condition and therefore pretty cheap. The entire front end can be totally destroyed if you can see that there are a lot of good parts on the rear end, and vice versa.

You may even find some surprises. I was once taking apart a parts machine and was surprised to find that only a couple loose bolts were holding the oil pan on. Hmmm . . . I surmised that someone had been working on that engine at some point, had quit, and just put the pan on with a couple of bolts to hold it on. That could mean a couple of things.

Either I was going to find a disaster in that engine when I got into it or, well, I didn't know what that "or" might be.

I unscrewed the bolts and dropped the pan and found that whoever had been working on it had installed new bearings in that engine and then for some reason decided it would be easier just to drop the job, maybe buy another, newer tractor. So he put the oil pan back on and walked away. Who knows how much later, I opened that pan to find a new set of main bearings, worth almost as much as I'd paid for the whole tractor.

There is also some profit to be found in parts. If you simply want to know more about old tractors but not get into repair, restoration, or rebuilding, why not buy an old wreck of a tractor, take it apart, and sell the parts on eBay or off a table at the next local tractor show? You won't lose much in the bargain, but I guaran-dang-tee you that you'll learn an encyclopedia's worth of information about what makes a tractor work.

Let's start with the nuts and bolts of the matter. That's the biggest part of a tractor's small parts, nuts and bolts. This is going to seem inanely basic to many of you—maybe even all of you—but I promise that we will move on quickly enough to much more complicated versions of whatever starts off looking way too easy to spend time on.

Okay, here goes: A BOLT is a threaded shaft with a HEAD on one end. THREADS are the little grooves that spiral up the shaft that the NUT is turned onto. The head of a bolt can be square, hexagonal, rounded, flat, oval, pan, grooved like a wood screw, an Allen socket head, or—and here's a great one for you—a "cheese head!" Just about the only kinds you'll find on an old tractor are square, hex, or grooved round or flat head. Occasionally you will also find an EYEBOLT, a bolt with no real head exactly but rather a loop through which something else might be threaded, strung, or tied. (Technically, I guess you could say that the most common kind of bolt you'll find on an old tractor is "rusty," "broken," or "stuck," but that's another issue altogether.)

Bolts come in various hardnesses, sizes, lengths, and strengths, sometimes indicated by SAE (Society of Automotive Engineers) index numbers. (On old American-manufactured tractors, you're not going to have to concern yourself with metric measurements.) Above all, the newcomer and even most veteran mechanics worry about the bolts' head type, length, and size—and this is really crucial—FINE or COARSE threads. The easiest way to understand the difference between these two bolt-thread types is to ask someone to show you both. No doubt about it, fine threads are, well, finer than the coarse threads. The coarse threads are coarser than the fine. There are a lot of reasons why there are two kinds—it's not just an arbitrary choice—but that's not really the point here. Just know that you can't put a coarse-thread bolt into a fine-thread hole. It just won't work. Nuts on old tractors are almost always steel, but occasionally—like on the studs holding cast-iron manifolds onto a block—you may find brass or bronze nuts.

There are even more kinds of nuts than there are bolts—square, hex, castellated, self-locking, captive washer, jet nuts, barrel nuts—but you'll only have to worry about the first three on that daunting list. And, of course, the now inevitable coarse and fine threads. What's more, you have probably figured out square and hex nuts. So the only mystery left is CASTELLATED. If you set a castellated nut down on your workbench top, you can imagine that it is the crenulated top of a medieval *castle* tower, you know, with the slots in it for defenders to shoot arrows from. On a castellated nut, the slots make the nut tighten down on the bolt so that it is less likely to work its way loose on moving items like rod cap bolts. More importantly, in places like rod caps, the bolts also have holes drilled through the bottom ends of the thread course; once the nuts have been tightened and torqued in place, a cotter pin (to be discussed below) is slipped into the slots on the castellated nut, through the bolt, and then secured by bending over the ends of the pin so it can't come out, and so that the nut can't turn on the bolt.

(Maybe this is the place that I should also mention that some bolts have holes drilled through the heads. This is so that a long wire can be run through a series of bolt heads and twisted tightly so the bolts cannot work loose on a moving part.)

As you can deduce and maybe even imagine on your own, nuts shaking loose on tractors is something of a problem. LOCK NUTS use various applications to keep a nut from turning off of its bolt or stud: collars, inserts, teeth, notches. All you need to know is that there are such things as lock nuts. And you won't find many, if any, on old tractors.

A JAM NUT is not really a *kind* of nut, but you *are* likely to find them on an old tractor. If that sounds like some sort of Zen riddle, it isn't. A jam nut is simply a second nut put on a bolt or threaded stock behind the primary nut. If you find two nuts one after the other on the same threads, the second one is the "jam nut." The thing is, if you tighten down the second nut against the first, those babies aren't likely to go anywhere without you putting two wrenches on them and twisting them apart with the same kind of force you used to put them on. A jam nut is a great way to keep something firmly attached.

Oh yeah, I guess there is one more kind of nut you will find on old tractors: the WING NUT. Wing nuts have, well, uh, *wings*. Two ears on either side of the nut let a mechanic more easily turn the nut off by hand, which is why you will find wing nuts in places where you are likely to want to turn the nut off: covers, hatches, latches, that kind of thing.

Another kind of fastener used to hold two pieces of metal together is the RIVET. A rivet is a metal shaft with a head that is put through a hole in two pieces of overlapped sheet metal. The end without the head is then spread and flattened, with a machine for that purpose, or simply with a hammer, so that the two pieces of sheet metal are held firmly in place by the head and the expanded end of the rivet. To remove rivets, they must be ground down on one end and driven out of the hole or drilled and pressed out. They are not re-useable, but they are inexpensive, readily available, and relatively easy to replace.

WASHERS are often found in association with nuts and bolts. They are usually little more than a simple metal disk with a hole in the middle. That's a FLAT WASHER and it is used as a spacer, a way to keep a nut from spinning on the threads, or to protect the part through which the bolt passes. A narrower washer—that is, with a smaller disk relative to the central hole— that is cut through so it does not make a complete circle is a LOCK WASHER. If you look closer, the ends at the split do not quite match up. That makes the lock washer actually a very short spring! The loose ends of that "spring" press against whatever parts are on either side of it, even just a touch *into* those parts, to keep the bolt or nut from turning. This is yet another system to keep things from coming apart on that vibrating, shaking, shuddering mess of iron called a tractor.

Washers are not always steel; even on old tractors you can find copper, fiber, composition, and rubber washers. Because of the intense vibration and the stress of holding a sheetmetal item onto a cast-iron base, on many tractors like my Allis-Chalmers WCs, the nuts on the studs holding the valve cover on the block are rubber or composition.

SHIMS, SPACERS, and BUSHINGS are a lot like washers: pieces of metal (mostly) that have holes through them and fit over rods, bolts, and shafts. Shims and spacers are more like washers, sometimes paper thin. Bushings are toward the tubular end of the scale. Shims and spacers put and maintain distance between parts and will range between microfractions of an inch to an inch or two in thickness or length. Bushings are tubes through which rotating rods turn—more like bearings than washers. You may want to be a little cautious here if your Master Mechanic starts talking about "acquiring some basic shim manufacturing stock." Home mechanics have found that commercial shims and shim stock can be quite expensive, but have also learned that beer cans—especially larger ones like Colt 45 malt liquor 24-ouncers—are not only often perfect for cutting shims but even offer a range of thicknesses. They are thinner in the middle of the can's "barrel" than closer to the "shoulders." If you have a micrometer—a rather fancy tool for measuring minute thicknesses—or know someone who has one, you can do some gauging. In most cases, the tolerances on old machines are great enough that you will be able to cut your shims and come pretty close to what you need by seeing how things fit. For example, shims are used to establish a proper fit of the rod caps, the shim spacer being inserted between the cap and the base of the rod. Most old-time shade-tree mechanics adjusted this spacing by trying to reach a fit loose enough so that the crankshaft still turned freely, but tight enough so that the turning is firm. A firm turning can be achieved by trial and error with shims.

A common tractor part that may look a bit like a washer, spacer, or bushing but that is actually quite different in appearance and function is the SEAL. A seal also fits around a rotating shaft—the axle, driveshaft, crankshaft—that is designed to prevent lubricating oil or grease from leaking out around the shaft. It is usually a fairly lightweight case with a leather, fiber, felt, or rubber liner that fits against the shaft. O-RINGS are a kind of seal; they are round rings rather than flat or squarish, sometimes even hollow inside. They fit in grooves in parts like cylinder sleeves and are partially crushed as the parts are put together, thus keeping liquids from moving across to places where they aren't wanted, like coolant into the oil or vice versa.

SNAP RINGS, LOCK RINGS, or C-CLIPS are also roundish bits of hardware, and since they do look a little like oddball washers, I'll deal with them here. Round shafts in engines and motors—valve stems, for example—are often held in place by small, springy clips shaped like Cs. Sometimes these clips are flat and have holes in each end of their C configuration where pins from a pliers-like tool can be fitted to spread them. Sometimes they are simply curved lengths of round spring steel. They are spread and slid onto round shafts and released so that they clamp down into the grooves in the shaft, thus keeping other parts from moving along the shaft or keeping the shaft from slipping through bushings. An invariable characteristic of C-clips is that they love to pop away and fall behind a workbench, where archeologists will find them in a couple centuries. Keep a box of spare C-clips on hand if you are going to work on old tractors. The terms LOCK CLIP and SNAP CLIP are usually used for larger C-clips.

There are other kinds of clips, sometimes also referred to as LOCKS, that can be put on items, or inserted into holes in items, to hold them in place. HAIRPIN clips look for all the world like old-fashioned wire hairpins, but they are larger and heavier. They can be snapped onto a groove in a round shaft like a C-clip, but they tend to be larger. Because of their size and shape, they can also be more easily pried off the shaft for easy servicing or replacement. While the true hairpin clip has two equally shaped "legs" that straddle the shaft, there are also hairpin clips that have one straight leg that fits into a hole in the shaft, while the other fits over the outside circumference of the shaft.

COTTER PINS, sometimes also referred to as COTTER KEYS, are very common fastening devices on old tractors. They are simply a length of steel folded in half, usually with a bit of a loop at the fold and with one leg a little longer than the other. The pin is inserted into a hole in the part that is to be secured—a throttle rod to a carburetor valve, or maybe into the slot of a castellated nut—and through the bolt onto which it is turned. Then the ends are bent over to hold the key in place. When cotter pins are removed from a part, they are always discarded and replaced; they are very inexpensive and easily available, which makes them a really common and handy part in any shop.

When someone refers generically to PINS, the item in question is more than likely a simple, straight, round piece of metal that is driven snugly into a hole made to fit it. Sometimes a pin is left sticking out either side of its hole to keep something in place. Sometimes its ends are hammered flat so the pin can't slide from the hole. When a pin is removed, it usually has to be destroyed in the process. The hammered and spread end has to be filed or ground off. The pin then has to be hammered through the hole and pulled out with a gripper of some kind like a locking wrench, driven through the hole with a pin driver or drift, or drilled out with a drill and bit. You don't reuse a removed pin. Believe me, its life is over once it's taken out!

ROLL PINS or ROLLER PINS are pretty neat items. They are fairly new on the market, so you are not likely to find them on an old tractor, but you might find a place where they can be used to replace an older, straight pin. Roller pins are round rods like a regular pin but instead of being solid, they are hollow rods with a slit along one side, which means they can be driven into a hole, flexing as they go, but fitting tightly. I don't trust a roller pin quite as much as a solid pin, but I do use them on places like cranking shafts.

WOODRUFF KEYS and STRAIGHT KEYS are, respectively, quarter-moon shaped pieces and straight lengths of square steel stock that are inserted into grooves cut lengthwise into a steel shaft. (In the case of the Woodruff key, the rounded part of the key is fitted into a rounded receptacle machined into the shaft.) When in place, the pins stick out of the shaft's surface a bit so that when the shaft is slid into its seat, the hole for it is not only bored for the shaft but also has a square channel cut to fit the key sticking out of the shaft. The function of these keys is to keep a shaft from turning in its receptacle or to lock two revolving pieces together.

The *Woodruff* part of the Woodruff key, by the way, refers to the inventor Frank Woodruff, who came up with this idea sometime in the 1920s in Rochester, Pennsylvania, although I have found theories that the device was actually invented by the Devil. One encounter with this nasty little device will lead you to suspect the same thing. Curiously, the Woodruff key has also become a symbol of importance for members of Rotary International. If you ask a Rotarian, I'm sure he'll be glad to explain the symbolism to you. While he's talking, make him look for the Woodruff key you lost under the workbench last week.

HITCH PINS are large rods that can be dropped through tractor hitches and drawbars to attach large equipment. They sometimes have handles and a hole drilled through them at the bottom so they can be locked in place but they can be not much more than a heavy metal rod with a head that keeps them from sliding completely through the hole. LYNCHPINS are smaller pins used to hold equipment in place, sometimes with sprung rings on the head that can be flicked over to prevent them from falling out of place. Lynchpins are often used to lock implements onto hitches.

A part can also be held in place, kept from revolving, or one revolving piece can be locked to another with a SETSCREW or LOCK SCREW. A hole is drilled through the outer element and threaded to receive the setscrew, nothing more than a bolt, but sometimes with a beveled surface at the end to fit into an indentation in the inner element. When the head of the setscrew—it can be square, hex, slotted, tooled for an Allen wrench, or even with a head like a wing nut—is turned in firmly, through the outer part and against the inner one, the movable one is set, that is, fixed in place.

Let's see: What else is there on old tractors that is used to hold one thing to another? Well, there are some clamps on old tractors, for example, HOSE CLAMPS. There are not a lot of hoses on some tractors. My Allis WCs have a sum total of three lengths of hose apiece: one at the top of the radiator from the block, another at the bottom, and a third carrying air from the air cleaner to the carburetor. But all three are held in place at both ends with hose clamps. Hose clamps circle the outside diameter of the hose, which has been slid over a metal fitting and tightened down to hold and seal the hose to the fitting. Older, inexpensive (and less effective) hose clamps simply use the spring constriction of a wire clamp to hold the hose in place; modern and much more effective clamps are tightened by turning a gearing part of the clamp with a wrench or screwdriver that applies slow but strong tightening pressure to make sure the hose is truly and firmly in place.

Okay, that pretty much takes care of small parts that hold things together. What else is on the list? I mentioned spring pressure on hose clamps in the paragraph above. Do I need to tell you that there are lots of springs in a tractor's machinery? Probably not. It doesn't seem likely that no matter how inexperienced you are with shops and mechanical work that you don't know what a SPRING is! There are big and little springs on a tractor. They are simply coils of metal, some pull and some push. All of them jump unexpectedly from place, hit you smartly around the eyes, and then bounce off to some place where you will either never find them or will locate them only when you step on them and crush them beyond further use. My own memories of springs are especially focused on the time I was prying a stiff valve spring from its place in a motor head with a screwdriver. It slipped from under the pry and hit me squarely in the middle of the forehead with the force of a shotgun shell, leaving a divot that I see in the mirror every morning and evening to this day. You can see why I don't want to spend a lot of time here talking about springs.

The most common PLUGS that show up in tractor conversations are spark plugs, but there are other kinds of plugs too. EXPANSION PLUGS are cups of steel thinner than the casting into which they are tapped, thus making a very firm seal with the larger casing around them. Expansion plugs are often used at the ends of things like camshafts that may eventually have to be removed from a casting but need to be sealed in place for many years. The shaft is put in place and then the expansion plug (or EXPANSION CAP) is hammered lightly but firmly into place. Nothing more than friction is needed to hold it in place.

The usual old tractor has a dozen DRAIN PLUGS scattered all over it: The bottom of the final drives, under the oil pan, under the transmission, in the PTO transmission, at the bottom of the carburetor. Some drain plugs have square extensions so the plug can be turned in and out with a wrench. Some are "innies" that have a square or hex hole in them so they fit fairly flush in their casting, but can be turned out with a square or hex tool. On my tractors, drain plugs are little more than common plumbing hardware.

GASKETS, gaskets, everywhere. That's the story of tractor mechanicking, right up there with stuck is stuck is stuck is stuck. When you attach one metal component to another and try to keep something from leaking in or out—coolant, oil, fuel, air, or compression—between those pieces of metal you're going to find a gasket. A gasket is a thin layer of cork, composition, rubber, metal, or paper, something softer than the two parts on either side of it that is compressed between those parts to form a seal. Sometimes a mechanic makes his own gaskets by cutting or punching them from sheet material, but sometimes they are too large or demanding to be homemade, the HEAD GASKET being the most common and obvious example. The head gasket fits between the head and the block. It has the job of keeping coolant, oil, and compression in the respective compartments. Most of the other gaskets on a tractor are not under a lot of pressure like the head gasket, so when you hear that a tractor or mechanic has "blown a gasket," it's almost surely a head gasket. It is often a combination sandwich of soft metal and heat and chemical-resistant materials. While a used head gasket can often be salvaged when dismantling an engine and reused, it doesn't take much of a dent or tear to ruin one. If an engine is at all important and the mechanic at all demanding, he's going to buy a new—and probably expensive—head gasket for it.

In other places on a tractor where there are not extreme pressures or temperatures, you may find a mechanic using a tube of gasket-forming goo, one of the wonderful benefits of modern chemistry and technology. Sometimes mechanics use GASKET DRESSING or GASKET COMPOUNDS, not to substitute for a material gasket but to coat it and ensure that it seals firmly to both sides. This can be particularly important in old machines where parts may not have fit perfectly to begin with, or after many years of use and abuse they no longer fit as closely as they should. But be careful!

Some mechanics look down on chemical gasket goo like a real Boy Scout looks down on using kerosene to start a campfire.

Right up there with gaskets and bolts in terms of frequency and importance in old tractors (or any other kind of machinery, for that matter) are BEARINGS. And like bolts and gaskets, they come forth in many forms—BALL BEARINGS, ROLLER BEARINGS, CONE BEARINGS, NEEDLE BEARINGS, THRUST BEARINGS—but the first three are basically the only ones you'll have to worry about in old tractors. But you will have to worry about them. Their function and positions in machinery mean that they are most vulnerable to wear and least likely to be serviced and maintained. That means they are the most likely items to need replacement when a tractor is rebuilt or restored.

Bearings are balls and rollers in cages that provide a rolling mechanism between two moving metal surfaces, or one moving and one static surface. That way, instead of two pieces of metal rubbing against each other, we have two pieces of metal moving over a rolling surface between them. Now, this is a terrific system for dealing with potential friction, but bearings have to be protected from dirt and weather, which means they have to be enclosed, which means they are easily forgotten, which means they are too rarely serviced. They should be oiled or packed with grease. Because they are often not adequately serviced, they often wear and fail. If they fail, they all too often have to be replaced because once they fail, we not only have solid steel rubbing on solid steel, we have loose pieces of metal rattling around inside, getting crosswise, banging up against each other, gouging, tearing, grinding . . . Well, you get the idea. The music of a failed bearing is for all the world like a bad day on a country music radio station.

Ball bearings are the most common form of bearing you'll encounter. They consist of a series of small steel balls in a cage. That works well, since a ball rolls pretty nicely, as we all know. Roller bearings are cages with rods of steel in them, offering more surface for the objects on either side, thus making them better for heavy-duty applications. Needle bearings are very small roller bearings; I've only encountered needle bearings in one antique tractor situation, so I don't think you need to spend a lot of time worrying about them. Cone bearings are nothing more than roller bearings in which one end of the rod is in a narrower circumference than the other; that is, the rods are in a cage shaped like a cut-off cone. (Perhaps I should also note here than a cone bearing often is seated in a BEARING CUP, the outside container for the bearing cage.)

I know it's all pretty confusing, but once you've seen and handled these items with strange and bizarre names, you will be tossing around names of hardware and parts without a second thought. You'll be the one scolding the green newcomer that no, you didn't mean a *piston* rod. You meant a *throttle* rod, and he should have known that since you were working with the carb, not the motor.

Oh? What's a THROTTLE ROD? It's the long, stiff wire that runs from the throttle control to the carburetor valve that gives the motor more or less fuel. I guess I forgot to tell you that. Sorry.

CHAPTER 8

TOOLS
AND SHOP

I had a really good friend, now gone, who was considered *the* man around
these parts and for many miles in every direction for magneto work. Now,
magnetos are a very special item when it comes to mechanicking with old tractors. Not many people can even tell you how they work, much less how they
should be repaired or rebuilt. My friend Dale could do that. He had a nice collection of interesting tractors, including an Allis WC road grader I wish I had. Now
and then I would take a magneto or two over to him and ask him to check them
out, maybe work on them if they were repairable. But as much as anything, I
liked to go into Dale's shop to renew my sense of priorities and perspective.

Dale's shop was an old automobile garage. It was built for cars made in the 1930s, I'd guess, because no vehicle after that period could possibly have fit through its narrow door. It had a dirt floor, a couple light bulbs hanging from the ceiling by their cords, and two small windows. There were a lot of drawers, bins, and boxes in Dale's shop, and that may have been where he hid a huge collection of expensive and specialized tools. Yet, in all the time I knew him and watched him work, I saw only two: a screwdriver and a Crescent wrench with a welded handle. Oh yeah, he also had a magneto tester he'd made out of a piece of PCV pipe and an old spark plug, but I don't think that really counts as a "tool." I can't help but think he probably had a hammer somewhere, but the only time I saw him pound on anything, he used the back of the Crescent wrench, which is probably why it had been welded.

My shop looks for all the world like a Sears Craftsman tool catalog display and cost me over the years roughly the same as what it must take to maintain a wife like Cindy Crawford. I have a lot of tools that seemed like a really good idea when I bought them but which I've never used. As my buddy Bondo points out, "Rog, when you die and they have the auction sale, the auctioneer is going to hold this stuff up and say, 'Here, you go fellas. Whatever this is, it's still in the original box!'"

All of which is to say, you don't have to get real fancy with your tools and shop to do some darn good tractor repair and restoration. I'm going to start with what I think are the most basic tools for a mechanic and dabble a little in the strange and exotic specialized tools, but remember, I'm not suggesting here that you *buy* this stuff because I am still thinking I'm writing for someone who wants to know what's going on in the shop and with that tractor rather than getting into the business himself. As if anyone can long resist the lure of great tools, a comfortable shop, and a fine old tractor that needs some lovin'!

Despite that warning, if you *really* want to learn about tools, wonderful textbooks are available free for the asking. Go to Sears and ask to be put on their mailing list for their Craftsman Tool catalogs, write to J. C. Whitney (www.jcw.com), Harbor Freight (www.harborfreight.com or 1-800-444-3353), or Northern Tool (www.northerntool.com or 1-800-221-0516) and ask them to send you their catalogs. Then spend some evenings in front of the fireplace contemplating the incredible variety of the things humans have invented for tinkerers. It *is* amazing.

If you want to torture your soul, find someone who keeps an account with Snap-on or Mac Tools and get an old catalog for those tool collections. You will weep, gnash your teeth, sigh, dream, sob, and whimper because the tools in these pages are so gorgeous. And so expensive. That's why you'll have trouble getting a catalog on your own. Snap-on and Mac don't generally have a lot of time or patience for pikers like you and me. I can't remember where I got my catalogs, but they are a good 7 or 8 years old. It doesn't really matter—the tools are still gorgeous. Now and then I order a Snap-on tool through the master mechanic here in town who has a full set of Snap-on tools.

I have a small Snap-on socket ratchet given to me by a friend and a set of thread chases I actually bought; I have one Mac combination wrench—a 7/8 I think—which I found in the road when I was walking home from town one day with the mail. When people ask me what kind of tools I use in my shop, now I can with all honesty say, "Oh, nothing but the best—some Snap-ons, Mac—and, well, you know, some other makes that I've picked up along the way." An unexpected benefit of this approach is that no one asks to borrow tools from me; no one in his right mind loans out Snap-on or Mac tools.

Although this chapter is not intended to be a plan for setting up the perfect shop, I would really be shorting you even as an innocent bystander if I didn't give you the very best advice I know about tools. First, get the very best tools you can afford. Which more often than not also means the most expensive tools you can afford. Sure, it's painful to spend 10 bucks on a $9/16$ combination wrench when you can buy a whole set of combination wrenches made in India for 10 bucks, but . . .

Take the test I once did on Linda when I wanted some good, new tools. Somewhere along the line, I had acquired a professional-grade polished Craftsman $9/16$ combination wrench from Sears, and oh man, did I want a set of those things. Yes, I would rather have had Snap-ons, but they're out of my reach financially, so the best I could hope for was Craftsman. Linda has always been very good about my expenditures but I guess I felt a bit of guilt about using family funds for something so frivolous. I mean, I already had some $9/16$ wrenches, so why would I need another one?

I went to the house and into the kitchen where she was working. I asked her to be patient enough to give me a minute for a little experiment. I handed her a $9/16$ combination wrench made in India and asked her to look at it and hold it a minute. She did. Then I handed her an el Cheapo $9/16$ wrench made somewhere else, Mexico, maybe. She held it, she looked at it.

Finally I handed her my one and only Craftsman wrench, the $^9/16$ professional model, fully polished. It didn't take her the full minute. She said without further comment, "Buy the wrenches." The difference and beauty is that clear.

Old-Tractor Rule Number Two: My buddy Dennis Adams, a farm boy mechanic, told me this early on. He said, "Rog, you save money by buying expensive tools. Thirty years later you'll be using the same tools. But if you buy cheapies, two years later you'll be buying them again." And as is so often the case with Dennis, he was right.

Old-Tractor Rule Number Three: You'll be using those expensive tools 30 years later; that is, if you aren't stupid and loan them to someone. If you do that, you will still be buying them again 2 years later. It doesn't matter how obvious the usual ethics of borrowing and returning are, how honest your friend or relative might be, how well intentioned all parties involved clearly are; you aren't going to get your tools back, or they are going to come back broken. The usual rules about borrowing just don't apply to books or tools for some reason. I once loaned a brand-new power washer to a professional mechanic and neighbor of mine, a guy I could trust. It came back broken. "Won't take much trouble to find the part and get that fixed," he said calmly as he unloaded my now useless washer. I never got to use it once. I loaned some chains to good, *good* friends, people I could trust; these guys who clearly knew better simply didn't care—hey, they weren't *their* chains!—so they tied knots in them to shorten them, the dumbest single thing you can do with a chain, and when they returned them hopelessly jammed up, they noted that I could just cut the knots out with a cutting torch and weld in new links. Thanks a lot, buddies. I loaned house jacks to a *relative* so he could jack up a sloping corner of his house and slip some new foundation blocks under it. This idiot decided that once he had the house leveled out, why bother with foundation blocks? Just leave the jacks in there and close up the opening to the crawl space! My jacks are still under there years later, rusting away.

Borrowers are all alike and not a single one of them can be trusted. *Do not loan out your tools unless you never intend to get them back* because that's the way it's going to go. Trust me; don't trust *them*.

Okay, you're standing around in a friend's shop, or your father's, or your spouse's, and the mechanic-in-charge says, "Quick! Hand me a wrench!" Well, a mechanic isn't going to say that because it doesn't mean much. What kind of wrench? What size wrench? You're not a mind reader! Chances are, he or she is going to give you more precise directions, and what I want to help you with here is understanding those more specific directions. Not only is the "wrench" probably the most common tool you're going to find in a mechanic's shop, but it is also one of the most richly varied tools in the box.

First, you need to know what kind of wrench he needs. In the most casual and amateur shop (and I use "amateur" in the very best sense of its Latin source: "lover") the word "wrench" means CRESCENT WRENCH. A Crescent wrench is widely adjustable to fit bolts and nuts of various sizes, which is why it is so popular. If there is a wrench in your household, it is most probably a Crescent wrench. It has a burled roller below the jaws that lets you adjust the size of the opening, which really makes it handy. An old-time mechanic may *say* that he wants a MONKEY WRENCH, but I'm betting he really wants a Crescent wrench because the old-fashioned monkey wrench, with its straight jaws and clumsy adjustment roller, has been long out of fashion for anything but hammering on stuff. And many an antique tractor toolbox still has a monkey wrench it for exactly that purpose!

In my mind and in the minds of a lot of mechanics, the adjustability of the Crescent wrench is also its weakness. It can slip more easily off a nut or bolt, and with a little wear it becomes loose and sloppy and almost unusable, maybe even dangerous. So most mechanics who are a little more serious about their projects prefer a wrench with a set jaw, which brings us to BOX END and OPEN END wrenches. There is also the marriage-made-in-heaven, the COMBINATION wrench, with a box end on one end and an open end on the other. Variation on the combination are the STUBBY combination that has a very short handle so you can get into spots that are too tight for regular length, or extra-length combination wrenches.

A lot of mechanics would argue with me about this one, but a wrench I wouldn't be without in my shop is the PIPE WRENCH. The pipe wrench is actually a plumber's tool. It has adjustable jaws that can be loosely tightened around anything round like a pipe (or, I guess, square or hexagonal, for that matter) and then as you push against the long handle, the flexible jaws tighten down on the object between them so you can really apply some pressure.

You want to be sure that the jaws of the pipe wrench are open in the direction you are pushing or pulling the handle, because the pipe wrench has a nasty reputation for slipping off what you are trying to turn if the jaws open back toward you, guaranteeing busted and bloody knuckles and experiments and adventures in creative cursing. In fact, those are good rules for any wrench: Pull when you can, but be sure your nose or teeth aren't in the way. If you have to push, push with your palm rather than a hand closed over the tool's handle. That's especially true of a crescent or pipe wrench. Be sure that the strain—your push or pull—is against the solid jaw of any adjustable wrench.

There are lots of other kinds of wrenches—strap, pipe, lug, flare nut, angle head, ratchet box, offsets—but if we go down that road, we'll be stuck here forever. For the more exotic forms of wrench, consider again getting a couple of those tool catalogs I recommended above and taking a look at them there. That way you'll even have illustrations to look at.

The first real tools I bought for my shop were a SOCKET WRENCH set. It is probably the tool I use the most to this day. If you are standing around someone's shop and are called on to fetch a tool while he's lying under a tractor dripping some icky fluid or another into his eye, my bet is it's going to be a "$7/8$ socket" he wants.

Now, are you going to stand there with no idea of what you're supposed to be looking for? Nosirree Bob! Now that you have read this book, you're coming into this situation fully armed and ready to fetch. A set of sockets gives the mechanic the advantage of having one handle with a wide variety of types and sizes of SOCKETS, fittings that are sized on one end to accept a projection from the handle so they are then firmly affixed to that handle, and sized on the other to fit firmly on various-sized nuts and bolt heads.

Of course, you know this discussion is going to get a lot more complicated before it gets any simpler. Mechanic-Now-with-Filthy-Oil-

Dripping-in-His-Eye is likely to add, "Make that a half-inch drive ratchet and an eight-point $7/8$ socket. Oh, and you might as well bring along a six-inch extension too. And a half-inch speed wrench handle while you're at it."

Well, great. Now what?

Let's start from the beginning. Grab a socket. Any socket. It looks like a small steel drum. On one end is a square hole into which the handle fits. It may be a quarter-inch, a half-inch, or three-quarters-inch square. (There are even bigger ones, but you're not likely to run across one in anything but a bridge builder's shop!) The size of that hole is the size of the DRIVE, or handle inserted into the socket.

Now look at the other end, also hollow. The hole there has a lot of sides in it, in fact, 6, 8, or 12 sides or POINTS. That's the hole that fits firmly onto the bolt or nut that you are going to try to twist. A **6-POINT** socket gives you the strongest grip on the usual 6-sided, hexagonal, or HEX nut or bolt; a **12-POINT** socket is for the same kind of nut or bolt, but gives up a little of its strength to give you some flexibility in which direction your handle will be pointing when you reach up under a motor, around the magneto, and try to undo that bolt waaaaay up in there. Sometimes the only way a 6-point lets you slide the socket onto the bolt head gives you no room at all to turn the handle. Maybe if you have a 12-point socket, you can get it onto that bolt with just a little more turning room. **8-POINT** sockets are for square-headed bolts and square nuts, and you are likely to find quite a few of those on old tractors.

A $7/8$-inch socket fits a $7/8$-inch nut or bolt, and a $9/16$ fits a $9/16$ nut or bolt. Nuts and bolts are measured in $1/2$-inch, $1/4$-inch, $1/8$-inch, $1/16$-inch, and even $1/32$-inch increments. This means you wind up doing some mighty fast calculating and wishing you had paid a lot more attention in Mrs. Grundy's mathematics class about fractions in junior high, but you'll quickly get used to it if you spend any time at all around tractors or in a shop. In fact, a mechanic with any experience at all can look at a nut or bolt and without measuring tell you exactly what size wrench he will need. It's a gift.

DEEP SOCKETS are exactly what they sound like: sockets that have deeper holes than normal for receiving the nut or bolt. These are really handy where you have a head deep in a casting like the block or if the bolt on which the nut is turned is long and sticks far enough out of the nut that a normal socket won't reach it.

Newer devices use the metric system, but I'm not even going to dignify that notion by putting it in upper case here. You won't run across much metric on an antique tractor. Nope, just good ol' American inches and feet, sixteenths and eighths. That's why working with old tractors is patriotic.

So, what happens when you have something to turn that doesn't have any sides or corners, something round but threaded on the end(s), something you don't want to ding up with a pipe or Vise-Grip wrench? Then what you might be sent to fetch is a STUD PULLER. Stud pullers come in two forms (at least for now—who knows what they'll come up with next?). One has a short barrel with a hole through it that fits down over a stud and clamps down on one side of the stud with an internal, toothed gear when you turn it in either direction. (It can be used to tighten or loosen a stud.) The other is a longer barrel with a deeper hole that fits down over a stud and, when turned, tightens down firmly the full circumference of the stud. I like the latter because it is less likely to damage the stud and seems to fit more firmly on the stud. From what I can tell, it has a bunch of loose rods in the barrel that tighten down on the stud from all sides . . . a much better arrangement in my mind.

Okay, now you know about sockets, that one end fits onto the nut or bolt and the other takes the handle. There are also different kinds of handles, each with a specific advantage for the mechanic, and each meant for a different job. Probably the most common handle used with sockets is the RATCHET. A ratchet handle lets you turn the socket in one direction, but then relaxes and lets you bring the handle back *without* turning the socket or taking the handle off the socket to reset it. You can imagine the advantage this gives the mechanic, especially in a tight situation. You don't have to lift the socket off that bolt or nut every time you give it a twist. To loosen the nut, you turn the handle firmly to the left, which, of course, turns the socket and the bolt or nut held firmly in its grasp. Then you don't take the wrench off the bolt or nut to return the handle to a position that lets you take another twist to the right. Nope, you just pull the handle back, it makes a little clicking sound *but doesn't turn the socket,* and you're ready to give it another pull to the left.

On the head of the ratchet, you will find a little lever or button that lets you change the ratchet to the other direction so that it will hold firm as you turn the handle to the right to tighten the bolt or nut and release on the back swing left. This gives rise to the most common and popular poetry of the mechanic's shop, "Rightie tightie, lefty loosie," by the way. You'll be surprised to note that even the mechanic who has spent 50 years working on machinery will occasionally pause for a moment as he affixes a wrench to a stuck bolt, look at it meaningfully, mutter something under his breath, and then apply pressure to the wrench. What he's thinking is, "Hmmmm, how does that go again? Oh yeah, 'rightie tightie, leftie loosie.' " Then he will return to the task.

My guess is that the next most common handle for a socket is a BREAKER BAR. It is a pretty simple device: just a handle with a swivel head onto which the socket is pushed. It is, in part, because of this simplicity that it allows the mechanic to put a lot of pressure onto the nut or bolt. There's not much to break, bend, or go wrong with a breaker bar. What's more, breaker bars come in a variety of lengths, the use of which depends on the amount of room the mechanic has to maneuver and how much he values his knuckles. I don't suppose I even have to tell you because you will learn quickly enough, but when applying pressure on a breaker bar (or any other tool for that matter), you don't want to be pulling it directly back toward your face. Nor toward that burr-edged, rusty old nut right in front of you. If something breaks or slips, you'll be showing off a new set of scars around the breakfast table the next morning. Before you start pulling or pushing any tool, think a moment about where your knuckles are headed if that bolt breaks.

I think the longest breaker bar I have in my shop is something like 24 inches. That's about the length of my courage. But some daredevils take the adventure even further and use a CHEATER on a breaker bar (or other wrench). A cheater (in some fancier circles called a DOGGING WRENCH) is a piece of pipe that slides over the handle of the wrench and considerably increases the amount of leverage you can put on it when you are dealing with an impossibly stuck nut or bolt—pressure, in fact, way beyond the manufacturer's recommendations. Mechanics who use cheaters often have nicknames like "Scarface," "Two-Fingers," or "El Stupido." When their wrenches come up for auction after the funeral, all the handles are bent.

You can't believe how many bolts and nuts there are on a tractor, and they all have to be turned a lot of times to get them off, and then at least that many times to put them back on. When dealing with bolts and nuts that aren't stuck and require a lot of leverage, you can save yourself a lot of time and effort with a SPEED WRENCH. A speed wrench looks like a crank. At one end, there is that square shank that fits into the socket. You install a socket on your speed wrench, push it onto the nut or bolt, grab the back end of the wrench and then turn the middle like a crank, making it possible to turn that nut or bolt a lot of times in a hurry. I love my speed wrench.

You're going to hear a lot in a mechanic's shop about the torque wrench. A TORQUE WRENCH or TENSION WRENCH is a kind of handle for sockets too but it has a very specific measuring function. Because it is a bit on the specialized side, some small, amateur shops won't have one. On the other hand, torque wrenches are becoming cheaper and cheaper and more and more mechanics are concerning themselves with the niceties of proper torqueing. Torque wrenches come in two main varieties. My favorite is a clicker. You set a dial on the handle to how much torque—turning force—you want to apply to whatever you are fastening and you slowly, firmly apply pressure. When you have tightened the item to the required FOOT-POUNDS you set on the dial, it makes a clear and loud click noise. Then you release the pressure, because you have TORQUED the nut or bolt.

On other torque wrenches, preferred by other mechanics, there is a mechanical dial or a needle that moves along a scale as you apply pressure, showing again the amount of force, or foot-pounds, you are applying. By the way, you don't have to guess how much torque a nut or bolt should have applied to it. Any technical manual for your tractor will give precise amounts of torque for the various nuts and bolts on your tractor that require torqueing, such as the rod cap nuts, head nuts, and bearing cap bolts.

I once asked the master Allis mechanic in this little town of mine how much torque I should use on the rod cap nuts of my WCs. He said to stick a socket onto a breaker bar, put it on that nut, and twist it until my belly-button stuck out about a quarter-inch. That's the way old-time mechanics did things.

Socket EXTENSIONS are solid rods and on one end, well, uh, you see, er, on the one end there's . . . Aw jeez, maybe it's time to stop pussyfooting around and talk about the facts of life so I can save some time and trouble here. On tools like socket wrenches there are two parts of connectors: There is the MALE END, which is the stickie-outie part or inserted end and the FEMALE END, which is the takie-innie part or receptacle. Whew. Okay, now that's taken care of. That's all my father ever told me about the facts of life and all I told my son and so it's all I'm going to tell you. If you need a further explanation, go ask your mother. The bottom line is, socket extensions are solid rods with a male end and a female end. You fasten the female end of the extension onto the male end of your ratchet, breaker bar, or speed wrench, and then you put your socket's female end onto the male end of the extension. That lets you work in very tight spots with the wrench handle itself out in the clear where you can turn it more easily. It *extends* the reach of your sockets.

There are various tools for measuring various things on mechanical devices. I think that if I had to settle on one, that would be a FEELER GAUGE, a thin metal leaf that is inserted between parts to measure the gap, or more precisely to make it possible for the mechanic to properly adjust the gap. Feeler gauges are most commonly found in sets that have dozens of blades like a pocketknife, but obviously with much thinner "blades." For example, a tractor motor requires a certain gap between the tops of the rocker arm and the valves. You insert the feeler gauge blade of the appropriate thickness—marked on the blade itself—and tighten or loosen the bolt at the end of the rocker arm until the gauge blade fits firmly in the gap but can still be withdrawn.

Probably the most common tool in American households next to a hammer or screwdriver is a pair of PLIERS. Don't ask me why they're a "pair" when it's only one tool. That's just the way it is. Like pants: singular at the top, plural at the bottom. Plain old household pliers are pretty handy for casual, occasional, light duty, but not all that great when it comes to heavy-duty, industrial-grade mechanicking. They tend to slip, they are tedious to hold in place for long periods, and they pinch fingers and palms. If you are sent to a mechanic's tool bench to get him some pliers, he's probably thinking of something more specific, like maybe NEEDLE-NOSE PLIERS—with long, pointy jaws that can reach into small places like engine galleries to retrieve dropped parts or into the eye of a cotter pin to get the needed leverage to pull it out of its hole.

Few shops these days are without LOCKING PLIERS, which are usually referred to by the brand name of locking pliers most associated with the tool, VISE-GRIPS. This drives the American Tool Company's lawyers nuts, especially when spelled the more common and incorrect way: "Vicegrips." This conjures up all kinds of possibilities for the creatively perverted mind. By means of a variety of leverage concepts, these pliers allow the jaws to be closely adjusted and then closed firmly in such a way that you get a very firm grip on whatever you're turning, or *trying* to turn; the tool then stays there firmly where you put it so you don't have to hold it. You can't imagine how convenient this is when you need, for example, to turn a nut with a combination wrench on one side of a piece of machinery while keeping the head of the bolt from turning on the other side. Fasten the locking pliers on the bolt so that it can't turn, and then you can proceed to feed the nut onto it and tighten it without constantly fighting a spinning bolt. A disadvantage of this arrangement is that once you get that nut turned, if you are anything at all like me, you tend to forget about the locking pliers. The eventual new owner of this same machine will find those pliers jammed up inside the side rail of the tractor some six years later when he is under there changing the oil. For those same six years, you will wonder what the heck ever happened to those clamping pliers you used to have. It's a normal and natural part of mechanicking, so don't worry too much about it.

You are more likely to find real workman's pliers in a mechanic's shop than run-of-the-household models. At my workbench, I have a variety of Vise-Grips and adjustable-jaw Channellock pliers, and I reach for them often.

Along the same shape and line are SIDE CUTTERS or WIRE CUTTERS. They look like pliers, but have sharp jaws designed for cutting things like soft wire rather than holding them.

Now that I have you confused about wrenches and pliers, let's take a look at SCREWDRIVERS. You'd think that would be simple enough; a screwdriver is a screwdriver, right? But no, the Tool Powers That Be have also managed to complicate *this* issue too. My dear old dad collected screwdrivers. He went to auction sales and farm sales and bought every interesting and unusual screwdriver that came up for sale. Every Christmas and birthday I gave him a screwdriver—for 60 years! His basement had pegboard on every square inch of the wall and on every square inch of pegboard there were screwdrivers, each one different from all the others. If ever there were an example of the ingenuity of man and his ability to complicate even the simplest concepts, it's the screwdriver.

But this is where working with *old* tractors is a real advantage. As mentioned earlier, there are, generally speaking, two main kinds of screwdrivers: SLOTTED and PHILLIPS HEAD. The slotted-head screwdriver is about as simple a tool as you can imagine since it's the one with the straight line. I can't imagine being a human being more than four years old and not being familiar with this one. If you press its point into a soft piece of wood, you get an impression that looks like a minus sign. The Phillips head, on the other hand, leaves an impression that looks like a plus sign. But, and here's the good part, you're almost never going to find anything on an *old* tractor other than bolts and screws with a straight forward, simple, good ol' American *slot screws* so you can save the Phillips screwdriver for your washing machine in the house. (The Phillips head screw was introduced by Henry Phillips in the mid-1930s because it provided a firmer grip for the driver and easier seating, squaring itself up at pretty much any angle, which made it much better suited for machine drivers. As you can imagine, the Phillips head screw really came into its own during World War II when American industrial production really went into its full blossom.)

The ALLEN WRENCH, that very simple little L-shaped piece of steel, is used to drive fasteners with a hexagonal receptacle in the top. It has the advantage of giving the driver a very strong grip, having a low or no profile, and being machine-driver friendly. It was trademarked by the Allen Manufacturing Company in 1943, which means it shows up on only later models of what we would call "antique" tractors. Because "Allen" is a proprietary name, you may find this tool listed under HEX tools in your catalog or L-HANDLE tools.

Of course, the fasteners on your washing machine probably won't take a Phillips screwdriver either. In an obvious effort to make it impossible for the home repairman to get into household appliances, yet do any repair work on them, manufacturers now use 10 or 20 different goofy fasteners that have holes in the top that are squares, five-pointed or six-pointed stars, images of Saturn, or the first six words of the Lord's Prayer—Torx fasteners and drivers, Dorx, Schmorx, Smurf, Turf 'n' Surf—you won't believe it. For these fasteners, you need a whole drawer full of DRIVERS, tools that look like screwdrivers but have the odd configurations on the business end. Most people working with old tractors, or anything else, don't fool with these, but you *may* find a set of HEX DRIVERS, things that look like screwdrivers but have receptacles that fit normal bolts and nuts. They're handy.

Another kind of driver is the SEAL DRIVER or BEARING DRIVER, a simple device that is pressed against a seal or bearing as it is being pushed into place. It is usually made of soft metal or plastic, so the fairly tender seal or bearing won't be damaged. A light mallet is used to tap on the driver and seat the bearing or seal. I usually just cut a piece of scrap wood to rough size, from the diameter of a dowel to a fence post, and use it. It's cheaper and just as efficient.

Surely—*surely!*—nothing could be complicated about a HAMMER! Hahahahahahahaha! (He sneers a sinister laugh!) Wrong again, greenhorn! When most people think of the word "hammer"—okay, most people *never* think of the word "hammer"—but let's just say that *if* most people thought of the word "hammer," they would think of a claw hammer or carpenter's hammer, the kind with a flat head on one side and a nail grabber on the other. Well, that's not usually what a mechanic is thinking when he says to you, "Hey, Dead Butt, why don't you make yourself useful and hand me a hammer!" (You can tell I've heard that directive before.)

While a mechanic worth his salt pounds on various pieces of machinery with just about anything within his reach—a wrench, beer bottle, stove poker, or a closed fist—if he specifically says *hammer* he probably doesn't mean a claw hammer. I'm betting he means a MECHANIC'S, CROSS PEEN, or BLACKSMITH'S HAMMER, usually a heavy hammer with a head that is flat on one side and with a horizontal wedge on the other. Or he means a BALL-PEEN HAMMER, flat on one end of the head, but rounded on the other ("peen" side), again useful for general flailing but also good for sheetmetal work. There actually is a process called "peening," tapping lightly on metal to relieve internal stresses, a process Linda has often suggested as a treatment for my own problems.

In my shop, I have a variety of heavy mechanic's hammers or MAULS, but also smaller ball-peen hammers for gentler tapping chores. *And* I have a few specialty hammers too: BRASS HAMMERS for pounding on things I don't want to damage or divot. Brass is softer than iron or steel, so if anything is going to get dinged, it'll be the hammer. It is also important to use a brass or bronze hammer when working around flammables; one spark can send your entire shop and you into orbit if you're not careful.

I have a COMPOSITION HAMMER with a soft rubber head on one side and a firmer nylon side on the other for more fragile parts that I want to carefully coax along without damaging them. RUBBER HAMMERS are exactly what they sound like and are usually used for pounding out sheet metal, but I have found them useful too in moving fragile internal parts. A DEAD-BLOW HAMMER is a composition hammer that has loose weight like BBs inside its head, which, for some reason of physics I can't explain because I don't understand them myself, means you get no secondary back-bounce when you hit something with it. It just goes *thud* and sits there. That saves you unintended dents in whatever you are working on or your nose, both useful concepts.

Because it's sometimes necessary to do some really heavy-duty pounding, most shops will also have a SLEDGEHAMMER or maul, a long-handled, heavy-headed hammer for full swinging when all else fails. I like to use a SPLITTING MAUL, usually used for splitting wood, for tasks like this. I *do* use it for splitting wood for my shop stove but I also use it for mechanicking because it has a tapered "blade" on the back side like a mechanic's hammer (except vertical, that is running up and down in the same direction as the handle). This can be used as a wedge for breaking loose a tractor's side rail from a front pedestal, for example.

I like to think I am the inventor of the LEAD HAMMER, or if there is any historical justice at all, the WELSCH-HEAD HAMMER. I found that I sometimes need real weight in pounding on nonetheless fairly fragile things like stuck pistons. So I melted some lead—old tire weights I found on my daily walks home from town with the mail—cut the top off an aluminum beer can, cut a hole the size of my hammer handle midway down the side of the can, and stuck the handle into and through the can. I had drilled a small hole in the handle an inch or two down from the top, and then screwed a screw into it so that it protruded an inch or so out of each side of the handle.

Then I melted and poured the lead into the can. Careful—it's HOT! If you try this, make sure there's no liquid in that can or it will instantly convert to steam and throw molten lead all over the place. Some of the lead may run out the hole you've made for the handle. This is obviously not a task for the weak of heart or careless of hand! The wooden handle smokes a bit, but the lead cools quickly. The screw through the handle assures that the head is firmly set on the handle.

On some of my lead hammers, I have peeled off the aluminum can once the lead cools. On others, I've just left it there. Aluminum is very soft, so it's not about to mar most things I'm pounding on. Lead is in fact so soft that you are going to find bits of lead flaking off as you use the hammer, and eventually the head will splay out enough that you are going to have to trim the excess off the head (save it for the next hammer you make) or burn out the handle, melt the head, and make a new hammer altogether.

You may find that those who love you won't let you do something as goofy as pouring your own lead hammers, or alternatively you may find that beneficiaries named on your insurance policies are overly enthusiastic about your intentions. Pouring molten lead to make your own hammerheads should not be a path lightly taken.

From here on, my choice of the most common tools found in a typical tractor mechanic's shop gets a lot tougher. I guess if I had to pick one more tool before my budget gave out, it would be a plain ol' ordinary cheap PUTTY KNIFE because that's what I reach for more than just about anything else. I can't imagine getting along without a putty knife at my workbench. I sharpen the front edge, and often one side edge, on my bench grinder (another crucial tool I will deal with soon), and use it constantly for scraping dirt, oil, and grease from parts. Nothing else does the job as well. I also have plastic scrapers, often nothing more than discarded windshield scrapers, discarded knives, old chisels for scraping edges, but number one on my list and on my bench is a putty knife.

Along the same line, I can't imagine having a workbench without a UTILITY or TOOL KNIFE near, one of those short (and very sharp) bladed knives that often have replacement blades inside their handles. I prefer the kind on which the blade is retractable so that no more of the sharp edge is showing than is needed for the job in question.

I swear, most of the activity in my shop is trying to get things apart. For that purpose, I turn first and most to my PRYBARS or CROWBARS, plain old carpenter's utility pries that can be inserted between the stuck parts and used to wedge them apart. My own pries range from a small nail-puller variety to five-foot-long rods made out of old automobile axles for really heavy-duty leverage.

While we're talking leverage, you may find yourself in a shop where there are PULLERS. Pullers use the leverage of the screw in various arrangements to pull off gears, bearings, seals, anything tightly affixed to a rod, axle, or shaft. Pullers usually have arms that are set around what you want to pull off and then a threaded shaft that is turned to push on whatever the part is attached. These things can generate a lot of pressure, so you want to be careful around them. Be sure to wear eye protection, which is always a good idea when you are working in a shop. There are two-arm pullers, three-arm pullers, and so on. Take a look in an automotive tool catalog.

Speaking of my tool bench, there are a couple things you should spot on any decent shop workbench, namely a VISE and a BENCH GRINDER (as opposed to an angle grinder, that I'll get to later). The vise is that big, iron clamp thing that you can tighten down on anything you want held solidly while you work on it. No shop bench is a shop bench without a decent vise. I have two on my bench, one at one end and another at the other. It's kind of a long bench for one thing, but also I like to have one big, mean ol' honkin' vise to hold the big stuff that will take a pounding, and a smaller one for lighter work.

The grinder is not much more than an electric motor with mounts on at least one—but usually both—ends of its shaft on which you can put a grinding stone for sharpening tools and putting edges on things like scrapers and, in the case of my grinder, at least a wire brush for cleaning things like rusty bolts, especially the threads. And as much as anything, for taking skin off my fingers and knuckles. It's the most successful way I have for losing weight.

Because there are so many nuts and bolts on a tractor, because doing any sort of work on a tractor requires removing them or replacing them, because they are often banged up to begin with or wind up that way after you've struggled to get them loose for an hour or two, next I would want a set of THREAD TAPS and DIES (also known commonly as thread CHASES) and a big can of THREAD CUTTING OIL in my shop toolbox. These are really tough nuts and bolts, often with slots across their threads to allow dirt, grease, rust, and bits of metal to be removed from the damaged threads as you force the stronger, harder threads over and through them. If you have a bolt or stud with bunged-up threads, you run a die or chase down the threads and then back off, and with some luck (and lots of oil to keep the cutting smooth and clean!) you will have bent, cut, or cleaned them enough so the part is immediately reusable. Same with a female thread. If you have a nut or stud receptacle that is damaged, you run a tap into it and hopefully that will clean it up enough to make it usable again.

I suspect that a lot of mechanics, professional and amateur, would disagree with me, but when you're working with old iron—rusty, stuck iron—I think that one of the most important tools you can have is a NUT SPLITTER. This is also the tool that as a newcomer you might be least likely to recognize. Not to mention that when your friend sends you to his tool bench to pick up and bring him a "nut splitter," you're likely to figure it's only a gag, right? A nut splitter is a pretty simple tool—a metal collar that fits over a stuck nut and a screw with a chisel end that you can turn down tighter and tighter until that chisel slowly bites into the stuck nut and splits it on one side. When that happens, the nut is usually ready to come off, and if it isn't, you simply turn the splitter and break the other side too. Sure, the nut is ruined, but you can always find another nut. Sometimes the most important task at hand is to get the original one off. When the wrenches and penetrants don't work, it's time to break out the nut splitter.

I know it's starting to sound like my shop is more dedicated to breaking things than putting them together, but when you're working with tractors that have been sitting in the trees, a barn, or a field for 40 or 50 years, well, sometimes getting it apart is 80 percent of the job. Therefore, some of the most important tools in my toolbox are:

A BOLT CUTTER, something that looks like a heavy-duty tree pruning tool, but with levered jaws so it can really put pressure on bolts or wire studs to cut them off when any chance of removing them intact has passed;

A HACKSAW, a bowlike thin-bladed saw specifically designed to cut metal;

FILES, not the kind for your fingernails but again specifically designed for cutting down metal. And don't be surprised if the mechanic in your life sends you to his bench to get him a "half-round bastard." It's not one of his no-good mooching buddies; it's a type of file!

PUNCHES, DRIFTS, and PILOTS, simple metal rods that let you place the point where you want the hammer's pressure. Then you tap the top end of the punch, pilot, or drift with your hammer, driving out the pin, rivet, or bolt you are trying to remove (apparently with some difficulty since you are now reduced to using a hammer). Sometimes these tools are made of brass so you can do your pounding without doing damage to the much harder iron or steel surrounding what you are trying to get out.

I told you I'd have to draw the line—actually, a lot of lines—as we worked our way around the shop, and this is one of them. I wouldn't even want to estimate how many different tools I have in my very small, very simple, very amateur shop—hones, ring compressors, spring compressors, spreaders, pullers—all kinds of weird stuff. As I have suggested before, what you really need to do is get hold of a tool catalog and spend a couple pleasant evenings sitting by the fireplace thumbing through it and looking at the pictures.

I guess we're moving toward power tools now, huh? My first choice for a shop power tool would be an ELECTRIC DRILL. I have not had a lot of luck finding an easily portable, reliable cordless drill even though that sure would be the handiest thing to have, so I use a plain, old-fashioned, unfancy electric drill with a cord. I do prefer a CHUCKLESS drill, which means you don't have to use a KEY to tighten BITS (the things that do the actual hole making) into the drill CHUCK, or receptacle that holds the bits. The key is a small-toothed tool that is used to tighten the chuck but that you can never find. (Hint: Tape your drill's chuck key to its electric cord, unless it is a cordless drill, in which case buy a bunch of keys and figure you'll lose one or two a month.)

Drill bits obviously come in different sizes to make different-sized holes but they also come LEFT HANDED and RIGHT HANDED. Most drills can be set to turn to the right (and therefore drill inward) or to the left (and therefore withdraw the bit from the hole) but there are also left-handed drills that are made to drill *in* as they turn left! Now, why would anyone want something like that? Well, the thing is, if you are trying to drill a hole in a stuck bolt or stud so you can get it out of the hole it is stuck or broken off in, when you drill into it with a left-handed bit, it is applying pressure in the direction that will get it loose, at least in theory.

It is the secret mantra of anyone who welds: The most important tool for welding is a good HAND GRINDER. It's "secret" because it's something of an admission too: a grinder can cover up a lot of welding mistakes by erasing them. At my workbench I have an ANGLE GRINDER, which is what most grinders are. That is, the axis of the grinding disk is at right angles to the body of the grinder; and therefore the diameter of the disk itself runs the same direction as the body of the grinder. These days, the disks on these things are tremendously abrasive, tough, and durable. They will quickly and easily grind down rough beads, rusty surfaces, stubborn bolts or nuts, and rivets.

It's not exactly a shop tool, but the lowly COME-ALONG (also known as a CABLE WINCH or CALF PULLER—for reasons you simply don't want to know if you are not already familiar with animal husbandry) is a must for any shop where you are going to have to move large equipment or pieces of machinery. This is a spool with cable on it and a ratcheted handle to turn the spool, tighten the cable, and then hold the spool where it is. There is a hook on one end that you can fasten with chain to an anchor—I have several permanent anchors in the cement floor of my shop—and the other end of the chain around the part, equipment, or tractor you want to move. That's the easy part. The hard part is pumping the handle to slowly, slowly, move what needs moving. I have written in other books that the most important thing about mechanicking is patience; one place patience is needed is in using a cable winch. A cable winch may not be fast, but it sure is effective.

Okay, now we're up—or down—to bigger pieces of shop equipment. Because they are bigger, they are also often more expensive. Since they are more expensive, they are less common in average, amateur shop settings. As has been my practice in these pages, I'm going to start with the devices I consider the most important to me, and most likely for you to encounter, as you become acquainted with the Zen of the Mechanic.

You can count on there being JACKS in a shop, that's all there is to it. But not the kind of flimsy bumper jacks that come in the trunk of your car. In a shop you need HIGH-LIFT or UTILITY JACKS, heavy-duty lifters on a solid base, with a heavy steel shaft, and a stout handle; HYDRAULIC JACKS, smaller bottlelike devices that use hydraulic principles rather than mechanical advantage to lift; SCISSORS JACKS, jacks that uses screws to pull together a scissors device and lift; or FLOOR JACKS, again hydraulic lifters but ones with added mechanical advantage and usually on wheels so you can move them with their long handles and slide them under whatever needs to be lifted. All of these have their advantages: The high-lift jack is tremendously strong, easy, and cheap to obtain, and it allows the mechanic work from the side of whatever he is lifting rather than crawling around under it. The hydraulic jack has a low profile, but a lot of power, and it can be fit under items where there is not a lot of clearance. The scissors jack is my least favorite since it is usually fairly light duty, but again, it has a low profile and can be slid into places where other jacks might not fit. The floor jack is really the mechanic's favorite since it lets you place it without having to crawl under the heavy beast you are trying to lift. It also works fast, has a ferocious lifting capacity, and is shop tough. Floor jacks used to be too expensive for the average shop, but now they are usually within range of all but the most modest of mechanics.

Of course, all jacks have their disadvantages too: The high-lift jack has a nasty habit of giving way to one side and letting whatever it is lifting drop to the ground—or your toe—whence their popular name, "widow makers." Scissors jacks break. Hydraulic jacks tend to lose their holding power as they get older. They also often have a small surface at the top of the piston where they do their lifting (which, to make things even more complicated, can be an advantage in a tight spot). Floor jacks are heavy and big. Any time you are lifting up something heavy, you are taking a risk. Be sure you are careful, and take as few and little risks as possible when using a jack.

Once you get whatever you are lifting lifted, you need something to hold it there. Never trust a jack to hold it up. That's the way a lot of mechanics die: by working under something being held up with a jack. What you need now are JACK STANDS. Nowadays, these are usually heavy-duty stands with adjustable height that can be changed quickly and easily by simply pulling up on the heavy cradle at the top where it is then held by a mechanical catch; to release the catch, there is usually a handle you raise. You can't do that when there is weight on the stand. That's good. You don't want a device that releases easily when there is weight on the stand. Beware of the mechanic who holds a jacked item with stacks of wood or cement blocks. Politely excuse yourself, dial 9, then 1, on the closest phone; wait for the crash to dial the last 1. Then stand outside to direct the EMTs to the shop.

One of the reasons I like working on old tractors is that they don't require men with, uh, full-bodied figures like mine to do a lot of bending over or crawling around in tight spaces. But sooner or later, if you are going to work on any kind of vehicle—even a tractor—you are going to have to lie on your back under that machine on a CREEPER. A creeper is a very low trolley that you lie on so you can roll under the tractor. Creepers come with various amenities—headrest, low profile, tool holders, adjustable backrest, four-barrel carburetor. Okay, I was just kidding about the carb, but take a look in a tool catalog and you'll see that inventors, manufacturers, and mad scientists really have managed to complicate this otherwise incredibly simply device in ways that will dazzle you. One word of caution—if you are a woman, country western singer, or aged hippie (like me), be careful rolling around on a creeper; I once got my hair caught in the wheels of my shop creeper and couldn't figure out how the heck I was going to get loose. It was only the desperation of the thought of being rescued by the local locos on our small-town EMT squad and the stories that would circulate the rest of my life about The Day Welsch Got His Hair Caught in the Shop Creeper that brought me to the point of tearing loose the snarled hairs and simply dealing with the short-term pain rather than the long-term humiliation.

Increasingly large, expensive tools that were once out of reach for all but the truly professional mechanic and fully-equipped shop are now becoming affordable for even the least of us tinkerers. Six or eight years ago, I splurged and bought a CHERRY PICKER (a.k.a. ENGINE HOIST), for example. That's a small derrick-like device with a winch or hydraulic cylinder on an arm that can be adjusted to reach out over an engine, transmission, head, anything heavy, and lift that heavy load slowly but surely, and hopefully safely. Cherry pickers are mounted on heavy-duty wheels so that the entire assembly, engine and all, can be rolled elsewhere so the engine (or transmission or head or whatever) winds up where it can be lowered onto a solid, firm stand, dolly, or bench.

For a while I was the only guy around here with a cherry picker, so I was beset by friends asking to borrow it. I have said elsewhere but I am more than happy to say again that no tools should ever be loaned from a shop—*ever*! Simply say no. Yes, you're going to make someone unhappy, but not nearly as unhappy as you are going to be when you never get your tools back or they return in considerably worse condition than they left. I was especially uncomfortable when I saw my expensive engine hoist leaving my yard in the back of a friend's pickup truck. (And yes, months later I finally had to go to his shop, load it back onto my truck myself, and haul it back to my shop where I could repair it.) I don't know what it is about friends and tools, but the two don't mix, believe me.

Thank goodness, cherry pickers have dropped steadily in price without losing much by way of quality, so now when someone asks to borrow yours, you can tell them you just happen to have a tool catalog right here that has a really inexpensive cherry picker on sale, and since you are using yours at the moment, you'd be glad to loan this buddy the catalog. (I'm betting that you'll find that as it becomes clear that you are not going to be generous in scattering your shop and toolbox across the countryside without a wife or daughter being left as collateral, you will have ever-fewer borrowers stopping by your shop. CAUTION: Be *especially* careful of anyone overly enthusiastic about leaving a wife or daughter as collateral. Be sure you have a signed return policy in hand before you make a trade like that. You may never see your shop equipment again.)

Everything that I have said about the cherry picker also goes for the ENGINE STAND and ENGINE DOLLY. An engine stand is a specialized dolly or cart with a heavy vertical frame mounted on heavy-duty wheels with lots of adjustments that allow pretty much any kind of engine to be bolted on so it can be easily and safely worked on from all angles, rolled around the shop, rolled over, whatever. An engine dolly is a small but heavy-duty, low, wheeled cart, again with plenty of adjustable arms, holders, bolt holes, etc., so an engine can be lowered onto it and rolled around the shop. Unlike the stand, however, a dolly does not allow the mechanic to turn the engine over or work on it conveniently. A dolly is simply to move the engine (or transmission, or head, blah blah blah blah) around, but not really to work on it as is the engine stand. I can't imagine doing serious mechanical work on engines without having both an engine stand and a dolly. They are still a little pricey for the modestly funded hobbyist, but they are high on the list of desirables even for tinkerers like me. (My tractor buddy Dick says he got his for about 30 bucks and it's a good one, so like many good things in this world, maybe engine stands are getting cheaper too.)

While I'm talking about dollies and other big equipment that is a bit painful for the hobbyist's billfold, I'll mention WHEEL DOLLIES. It took me a while—years—to convince myself that I really needed wheel dollies for my shop. I'm glad I have them now. I don't use them all that often and I suppose there's still some question about whether they are worth what I spent for them. These are very heavy-duty wheeled pans that can be slipped under a tractor's or car's wheels. You jack up your car or tractor, slip the dollies under the wheels, and lower the vehicle down onto the dollies. Now you can move the vehicle you are working on with little more than a pry bar or come-along, maybe even with a couple of heavy-duty helpers pushing on the machine if your shop floor is smooth and even. As you can imagine, wheel dollies can really be useful when you have to move a vehicle around—like sideways—in a small, tight shop, or when you are working with a real piece of wreckage that is reluctant to take any sort of movement suggestions on its own wheelage. (I just made up that word too.)

When someone really gets serious about mechanicking and is either single, stinking rich, or has developed a successful system of double accounting so the spouse has absolutely no idea what kind of money is flowing out the shop windows, you are likely to find some really big, expensive, and really grand equipment like an air compressor, a welding outfit, or—oh man, the fantasies!—a plasma cutter! I wrestled for almost a year with what I wanted to add to my tools most—a welding outfit or a compressor. I think I made a wise choice in deciding on a compressor, but I made the mistake of getting a small one that was totally inadequate for even my modest needs. That, in fact, has been a common error of mine. While this is not meant to be a primer in starting a shop of your own, let me give you a bit of advice about that anyway: The advice about doing something right if you are going to do it at all is just as true for big expensive things as small, inexpensive things. But somehow it's easier to figure that you'll go all out and spend $20 for a really good wrench instead of settling for a $6 cheapie, but it's tougher to take the step of spending $300 for a big shop compressor rather than $125 for a dinky portable unit on wheels. Don't do it. A small portable compressor has its uses, but if you are going to use a compressor for shop work, get a full-size, quality compressor.

An AIR COMPRESSOR is a small air pump mounted on a big, heavy tank. The pump packs air into that tank and holds it there for you to use when you need it to power hand tools, everything from an impact wrench for breaking loose nuts and bolts to cutters, grinders, plasma cutters, and burr grinders. Again, take a look in a good tool catalog and you'll see all the things you can hook onto an air hose. Probably the most common use for a shop air compressor is nothing more than an air gun on the end of an air line from the compressor, to blow dirt away from parts and projects. Nothing works like a good blast of air for a job like that. I don't use my big Sears Craftsman air compressor very often, but when I do, I'm sure glad I have it. I still hope Linda never notices it sitting out there and wonders where the money to pay for it came from.

Eventually it became evident that I was indeed going to have to have a welding outfit as well as the compressor. At least that's what I said in between sobbing and begging when I told Linda. As always seems to be the case with things like this, deciding what kind of WELDER you want and need is not always a simple decision. I knew absolutely nothing about welding—I still don't know a lot—and as was the case with everything else around here like the compressor, my first choice was probably not the best. The thing is, to me "welding" was an electrical operation with lots of hot sparks flying around, a big helmet, heavy gloves, leather apron, that kind of thing. I guess I saw too many World War II movies when they were building Liberty ships with ARC WELDERS or STICK WELDERS—the electrical setups that melt metal and join it with the intense heat of an electrical arc. Welding is an inherently dangerous process, not only because of the intense heat but just working with electricity has its obvious hazards. Also, the bright light can damage your eyesight if you don't have the right kind of protection. Even if you are just standing around a shop watching someone else weld, never look at the arc without wearing suitable eye protector goggles or a mask meant specifically for arc welding. You also don't want to stand too close with bare skin showing for long or you will exit the shop with a sunburn from the arc's radiation without the usual pleasures of lying around on a sandy beach with a daiquiri in your hand.

A GAS or ACETYLENE WELDER or TORCH uses the heat of a flame instead of an electrical arc to melt and join pieces of metal. A system of valves and hoses release acetylene gas and oxygen from a pair of heavy tanks and joins them in one of a variety of nozzles that are used to heat, join, or cut steel. I find it a little tidier—not so much by way of sparks and hot metal dropping into your shoe tops or overall cuffs—but still pretty demanding when it comes to learning how to adjust the flame to your best advantage. As with arc welding, if you are kibitzing in a shop, don't look at the flame or stand too close to the work. You'd be surprised how easy your socks can catch on fire.

Neither an arc welder nor a gas setup is a bad choice for a beginner. Both are good ways to learn about welding and quite a bit of the information gathered is useful in both techniques. No welding setup is cheap, but you can sometimes find used arc or gas welders at a reasonable price. The reason for that is that no one wants them anymore. At least, not for the amateur shop or for the mechanic who wants to do some welding without becoming a full-fledged expert at it. I started with an arc welder and got to be fairly good with it, at least for my purposes. But then I wanted to do some cutting and was told that what I needed for that was an acetylene torch, so I went ahead and invested in the tanks and equipment for that. Again, not the most brilliant move I ever made.

Then a friend gave me a WIRE-FEED WELDER (Firepower 120 MiG welder) and it was like going from my first wife to my second. Holy cow! This was like heaven! I couldn't believe it. And I couldn't believe I had ever fooled around with sticks or gas. With an arc (a.k.a. "stick") welder, you fasten one end of the electrical circuit with a cable and clamp to the piece of steel you are working on, and you put a rod of metal coated with FLUX (a substance that permits the metal to melt, flow, and stick to what you are trying to join together) in a clamp on the other cable. Holding the flux clamp, you touch it to the steel, and the spark between the two melts the stick and the two pieces you are joining, thus making them all one. With gas, you hold a rod of metal coated with flux in one gloved hand and slowly feed it into the ferocious flame, joining the two pieces. But with a wire-feed welder, you clamp a cable to your work piece, hold a hand-gun near the work, and when you pull the trigger there is not only an arc for the heat necessary to welding but also a strand of wire coming out the end of the gun at exactly the right speed for whatever you are welding, and—here's the best part—a shield of gas that does the same job as the messy flux of stick or gas welding. I found that I was doing a better job of welding with my wire welder almost at once than I had been doing with an arc or gas welder after years of practice. Believe me, if you are going to remain a hobbyist, an amateur, or a tinkerer, consider a wire welder.

I'm an even worse solderer than I am a welder, so I don't have much to offer by way of advice on the topic, but briefly, SOLDER is a soft, lead-based alloy that melts at a relatively low heat and so can be applied to join metals or seal holes in metal with little more than a hot electric iron, a SOLDERING IRON. It has the advantage of also working for joining copper pieces, which is what oil and gas lines and radiators are made of. Solder also has the advantage of not requiring a gas or electric *flame*; imagine that you have a gas line or gas tank with a pinhole in it and you want to seal that hole up. So you drag out your gas- or arc-welding outfit. You can kiss your shop goodbye, and probably your widow too if you do that. It doesn't matter how dry that gas tank or line seems, or how long it's been sitting in the sun drying out. You don't want to approach it with a flame. Solder is what you want, and even at that, you want to use every precaution you can to avoid a really big explosion. As with welding, oxidation is prevented on work materials with the use of a special soldering flux. Solder comes in a variety of forms, some with various kinds of flux built right into it or on it already, but that's more than you need to know at this point. Ask an electrician or plumber; they use solder all the time and know all about the stuff.

It's not easy to *cut* steel with a stick welder—it can be done, but it requires some real skill—and not at all possible with a wire welder. So, if you go the route of a wire-feed welder and still have cutting needs, especially if you are left a lot of money by a rich uncle or find a suitor who is a Saudi oil sheik, take a look at a **PLASMA CUTTER**. I have a Firepower FP-25, a small, compact, portable unit that has yet to fail its assigned tasks. A plasma cutter uses a small, relatively cool electric arc to do its cutting, but—*but*—it also blows out around that arc a blast of compressed air (which means you will also need a compressor), which means it cuts like crazy! Even if you will never buy one, you should visit a friend who has one and give a plasma cutter a try. You'll be astonished. It cuts so clean and cool that you can write your name in a sheet of 1/8-inch steel as if you were writing with a ballpoint pen. I have one and I absolutely adore it. I told Linda it is a "cardiac restorative generative pulsolator" that I can use if I ever have a heart attack in the shop to bring myself back to life. Yeah, I don't think she bought it either, but she probably figured that I was going to get one sooner or later no matter what she said, so she just settled for a steak dinner up at the town tavern and I got my plasma cutter.

My personal choice in equipment and supplies over the years has been Firepower. Your own selection will probably depend on price, availability, advice of friends, and just plain ol' serendipity. Modern technology means that even the worst of equipment is a big step up from what our fathers and grandfathers had to put up with, but I have had very good luck with Firepower products.

As with everything else I've discussed in these pages, welding and the equipment for it are far, far more complicated and varied than I can discuss in a few pages. There are rosebud nozzles, cutting torches, powder torches, on and on, so if you are going to get serious about welding, go ahead and get serious about welding. Get the books that deal with precisely what you are interested in, take some lessons from an expert, get some advice, and, most importantly, practice, practice, practice until you feel confident in working with scrap metal before taking on something serious. Take a class at your local community or tech school or, as I did, simply ask a local welder to give you some lessons. I offered to pay my old pal Don to teach me welding, but he was glad to do it just for my appreciation of his skills—and a couple of draws over at the tavern after each lesson.

Even though I have a pretty full set of welding equipment, I also keep a simple PROPANE HAND TORCH, the sort that you can pick up for a couple dollars at any hardware store. While it does not generate enough heat to weld, it is very useful for heating small pieces of work, like stuck nuts and bolts that you need to heat to break loose.

Just as is the case with small tools, there is a never-ending inventory of large equipment that any mechanic winds up lusting after, and maybe eventually acquiring. I love rebuilding engines, for example, so I wind up with lots of valves and valve seats that need to be ground down to make them clean and even so, they form a firm seal when those little gasoline fires are going on in the cylinder. Well, VALVE and VALVE SEAT GRINDERS are expensive and specialized pieces of equipment, but I watched the newspapers and eventually I found a valve grinder for sale when a big automotive repair shop went out of business. Not long thereafter, I saw an ad in our local newspaper for a valve seat grinder a retired mechanic was selling. I got both machines for about what I would have paid to have two sets of valves ground in a commercial shop.

As more and more amateurs like me—and maybe you—get into this activity, the prices for equipment are dropping. I waited quite a few years before I got a SANDBLASTER—nothing fancy, a simple tank that holds an abrasive (anything from ground walnut shells, no kidding, to, well, *sand*) and various devices and valves that control the force of the air blast and amount of abrasive. Hook this up with an airline to a compressor and you've got a tool that cleans dirt, rust, and grit off of parts with astonishing speed and ease. Prices on them came slowly but surely down, and then there was a sale, and now I have one of those tools too.

As I have spent weeks writing these words and pages, I have tried to keep my focus on my goal by imagining again and again the most likely scenarios of a newcomer—you—being sent by some grizzled old shop veteran to fetch something from the workbench or toolbox. This primer serves the purpose of keeping you from making a dang fool of yourself by mistakenly bringing your friend or kin a three-arm gear puller instead of the left-hand quarter-inch drill bit he asked for, thus branding you forever amongst the boys up at the town tavern as "Don't-Know-a-Puller-From-a-Driller" Welsch, a fate much crueler than you might imagine. In short, I see myself in these pages as an angel of mechanical mercy, doing what I can to save the innocents from lives of agony and humiliation.

Not as easy as you might think. For all the convoluted descriptions, explanations, outlines, and cautions I've offered so far, it all pretty much falls apart right here and now. The honest fact of the matter is, in maybe 9 out of 10 cases, when your mechanic buddy sends you to fetch him something, it won't be quite as I have described—a quiet, calm, clear instruction of exactly what he wants and needs. No. He's not going to turn calmly from the stuck oil plug he is going about carefully and scientifically loosening, adjusting a floor pan carefully so not even the slightest drop hits his carefully scrubbed shop floor, turning the work lamp just so, so he can see precisely what size tool he is going to need.

No, he is not going to say anything even remotely like "My friend, would you mind stepping over there to my toolbox, opening the drawer labeled Drivers, Hexagonal, and bringing me a $7/16$-inch driver, the one with the blue handle? It should be in the holder immediately between the $13/32$- and $1/2$-inch drivers. I have them all labeled on both the holder and on the handle. Be careful not to smudge any dirt on that drawer handle now!"

No, what is far more likely is that you will first notice some immediacy in the problem as filthy oil spits out from the bottom of the engine, stinking for all the world like something besides the magneto has been dead for years in that engine. As the oil splashes off his forehead and onto the lamp, blowing the bulb and filling the shop with acrid oil and the sounds of cursing in what may be Croatian or Mayan since your friend's mouth is now also full of oil, you are more likely to hear something like "@#$%$#@ it anyway. Don't just stand there with your finger up your nose, you idiot! Get me that . . . that . . . oh dang it anyway, you know what I need! Get me that [fill in word here from choices below] and throw it under here just as hard and fast as you can! And while you're at it, take off your shirt and mop up the oil and water that's running onto the tech manual I just dropped. *Move, or are you too busy laughing to save your own sorry rear before I come out from under and stuff you into the woodstove?"*

Terms for possible insertion in brackets above, as indicated:

Thingamabob

Dealywacker

Whatchamacallit

Doodad

Thingamajig

Dinkus

Turnie thingie

Black-handled sumbisquit

Youknowyouknowyouknow

Broken-handled gadget that just fell behind the bench

Etc., etc., etc.

This confusion is not simply a function of the obvious and sudden need that frequently surrounds shop activities. This is something very few other authors have had the courage to take on, I might note. The thing is, if you were to count each and every tool in your typical amateur mechanic's shop, you would find only about half of them listed in a commercial tool catalog because only about a half of them are what you would think of as a commercial tool. Or what you would call by their actual names because it would be, well, just too German.

You see, Germans never call anything what it really is. They can't. If they did, they wouldn't have any time left to invade Denmark. Now, brace yourself because this is going to sound an awful lot like that educational stuff you avoided so carefully in high school, but believe me, I'm taking you somewhere with this. I don't suppose you know the German word for the guns that shot stuff up into the air to stop Allied bombers during World War II, do you? Of course you don't. Even if you do, don't bother to try to say it because we don't have time. It's *Fliegerabwehrkanonen* or *Flugzeugabwehrkanonen*. That translates to "Flying machine defense cannons." Obviously, this wouldn't work. You are a German and you spot a B-25 approaching with a load of bombs. You spring to the radio and scream, "Breaken Sie Outen die Flugzeugabwehrkanonen!" By the time you got the orders out, the planes were already over Dresden. So, you shortened it to "**Fl**ugzeug**a**bwehr**k**anonen," or *Flak*.

Or you were taken captive but wanted to explain to the GI dogfaces with rifles up your nose that you're just a common soldier yourself and not one of the Nazi swine who engineered all this stupidity. "I am NOT a member of the *Nationalsozialischedeutschearbeiterpartei*," you shout. By which time, you are dead and the GIs are back home celebrating V-E Day. So you simply shorten it to *Nazi*. Then you're back to eating bratwursts at Oktoberfest and singing drinking songs with American tourists, just that quickly.

Same thing with mechanics. Imagine being in the scenario described above and telling your eager assistant Igor, "Quick! Go to the workbench and grab me that old-tablespoon-I-lifted-from-the-last-sports-banquet-over-at-the-high-school-and-bent-into-an-L-shape-so-it-just-fits-an-Allis-WC-oil-plug-slot!" Won't work. It's easier to yell, "Hey, Leadfoot! Throw me that thingamajig over there by the dealiebopper!" Once you've had a little time in a shop and a little practice working with your mentor, you will know *exactly* what he means. It is then satisfying, and just a little eerie.

One of the great secrets of any shop is how much of the equipment is post-production adaptation: that is, tools jury-rigged out of all manner of other things never meant for the task they now serve so well. You will be amazed. There are three general categories: 1) Tools meant for a completely different application but now serving the mechanic as tractor tools, 2) Tools that are actually meant to do something else but have been adapted to shop use—more often than not common household items now rejiggered for shop use, and 3) Tools made from scratch by the mechanic for a specific use in his shop or for his tractors. What's more, I personally consider this a kind of moral hierarchy. That is, I think tools for one job that are simply used for another is a fine idea, and inventive to a degree, but man, to devise and fabricate your own tools, now, that's really something.

Let's start at the beginning, tools from other trades. I am not a woodworker, for example. But I have wood chisels in my tool drawers. I use them in ways that would make a woodworker cringe or cry: I scrape grease and dirt with them, pound on them with hammers until the handles split, and grind them down until they disappear in a pile of metal fragments under the bench grinder. I use splitting wedges from wood chopping as devices to pry side rails away from front pedestals.

Perhaps my favorite such adaptation is from my friend Jim Cossaart, a dentist now in New England. When I first met him, he was a windmill repairman in northern Kansas, so his transformation into a dentist seemed a natural progression to me—both windmill gears and people have teeth. I imagine that's why he didn't so much as wince when I asked him if he ever had any old, broken, worn, damaged, or obsolete dental tools he might send me. Within days I had a bundle of probes, pries, points, stabbers, glommers, stickers, scrapers, jabbers, and, well, thingamabobs. A whole drawer of my toolbox full. I use Jim's tools for pulling O-rings and seals, for cleaning small parts, for, well, for exactly the same things they were good for in their previous life with Jim. Now I cannot imagine being a mechanic and not hitting up my dentist for all his old tools.

Next, we have items that are not tools but have become tools. Nothing leaves this house without making at least one pass through my shop. That includes all cloth goods (although Linda does adamantly refuse to submit her discarded dainties for use as shop rags), anything that can hold anything (cottage cheese and butter tubs, spray or squirt bottles, coffee cans, boxes, plastic bags, whatever), anything that can be used to scrape, pry, or pound (plastic flatware from the drive-in, discarded beauty and hygiene supplies like toothbrushes, eyelash curlers, things women use for magic bathroom spells, pots without handles, lids without pots), or anything that could conceivably be thought of as a shop "supply" (clothes hangers, filters and strainers, odd gloves, and toilet plungers). It can all be used in the shop—all of it.

It is a *huge* and painfully feminine mistake to ask the question, "What are you going to use *that* for?" There is no way to know what you are going to use that for until the time comes to use it. If you didn't save it for just this moment, you don't have it when you need it. When you do need it, you'll probably be either too embarrassed or too panicked to tell your shop visitor to hand you the toilet plunger so you can use it to bang loose a stuck piston, so you'll just yell: *"Hand me the @##$%&%$##@ thingiemabob from over there by the workbench, will you, or would it be too much trouble to ask you to get off your dead rear end and be useful?"* Now, see how that works?

The tools real mechanics are most proud of are the products of their own ingenuity, specialized items they have had to make for themselves because 1) they needed this particular tool at once and didn't have one, 2) they couldn't afford the commercial version of the same thing, or more likely 3) no one made what they needed and so they just made one for themselves. Of course, these are also by far and away the most difficult tools to talk about because they have no official names. They exist only in this one shop, not in the certifiable world of shop mechanicking.

I think that one of the reasons I have a special affinity for homemade tools is that some extra-clever American craftsmen working in their shops have come up with tools I love, and gotten rich in the process. Vise-Grip and Channellock tools were both the products of village blacksmiths tinkering and doodling in their small shops.

For example, imagine that you have a stud, threaded on both ends, that you need to turn into a hub or block. You've cleaned everything, run a chase over the male threads, a tap into the female receptacle. You've put a little dab of grease on everything to make this a smooth operation and you're all ready to go. But you *are* working with old iron, so everything is not perfect. The stud is turning a little hard. Now, you could put a pipe wrench or locking wrench on that stud and turn it in, but you worry about scarring up the stud's shank with the wrench's teeth. You sure don't want to bung up those threads! So how do you get a grip on that stud so you can turn it easily but with some leverage?

Aha! There is Roger Welsch's Almost-Patented BLIND NUTS, nuts of various sizes onto which I have welded smaller washers so I can turn them onto a male thread only so far before they hit the dead end and can turn no further . . . *without turning the stud*! Now I never work at putting in wheel studs, head studs, or manifold studs without proudly going to my bin of blind nuts that make the job easy.

Or, how about this? There is a constant need to turn an engine's crankshaft, and thus raise and lower the pistons and valves while it is off the tractor and mounted on an engine stand. It's not easy to turn over an engine, especially when it's been rebuilt and things are tight and stiff. Fitting a hand crank into the crank fitting is way too clumsy. So? Well, I had my mechanic friend Kenny weld a short piece of pipe with cross pegs that fit into the hand crank fitting on an Allis WC engine on one end and a large hexagonal nut on the other. That way I take this easily handled item, stick it into the crank receptacle, and then with a box wrench that fits the hex nut, I can easily turn the engine over, even in the tight confines of an engine stand.

I'm a genius! I'm a mechanic! I'm an engineer!

During my decade of enjoying hours in my shop, one of the most helpful and welcome innovations has been the development of wonderful new chemicals specifically designed for folks like us. Now, to be sure, to some degree it's not the world of mechanicking or even the world of science that has changed, but the simple process of me slowly learning what the heck is available for us out there on suppliers' shelves. For years I used kerosene (even gasoline!) and mineral spirits to clean my hands before I returned to civilization, uh, the house from my shop. As a result, I smelled like the shop floor rather than my own lilac-scented self and my hands took on the texture of emery cloth.

Well, no more! There is a wide variety of absolutely super hand CLEANSERS for the shop—cream and liquid, orange, green or white, with cleansing grit or without, in dispensers, tubs, or jugs, scented and unscented—and almost all a world beyond gasoline! The stuff is miraculous, no kidding. It is fast, effective, and much easier on the skin (although I have also taken to applying my favorite hand cream "Working Hands Crème—1-800-275-2718—even after using commercial cleansers for those baby-soft hands that Lovely Linda so appreciates).

When it comes to cleaning parts, science has also raised its helpful head. I still use kerosene for rinsing and cleaning some parts because commercial engine and parts cleaners can get to be pretty expensive when you're cleaning a lot of parts or really big ones. Nevertheless, any commercial parts cleaner is useful, especially when bought in larger containers. (I'm thinking of gallon or even 5-gallon containers, but if you have the room and money for a 50-gallon drum, more power to you!) These compounds are designed especially for cleaning purposes and they do things kerosene was never meant for. Also, don't forget the very best universal solvent of all: water! Hot water and dishwashing soap is my first and final resort for cleaning in the shop.

For really tough problems—baked-on grease like that on a head or valve parts—I like plain old commercial spray-on oven cleaner. It is really harsh, however, and should never be used on aluminum or babbitt parts. Be sure to wear rubber gloves and goggles when using this stuff. It really is dangerous, but it does work when and where nothing else does.

The same is true for shop SOLVENTS and PENETRANTS. At the tractor chat sites on the web and in conversations in local mechanics' shops, you'll hear talk about various substances used for breaking loose sticky parts, freeing stuck pistons, dissolving grease, rust, dirt, iron rot, whatever. You'll be astonished. Melted paraffin, Coca-Cola, olive oil, and vinegar (save this one for the salad bar, please!), Drano, or lye (if you soak stuck aluminum parts in this stuff, you won't have to worry about them coming loose—think about replacing them!), brake fluid, even Jack Daniels Green Label, which may loosen stuck parts in the mechanic, but shouldn't be wasted on rust and corrosion.

Skip all the home remedies for stuck stuff. Whatever money you save is still wasted. These things may work to some degree (especially, I am told, the paraffin trick) but you are always safer with penetrants designed by chemical engineers who specialize in molecular science than wacky notions cooked up by some yoyo who's spent way too much time leaning over an exhaust manifold. Modern penetrants are amazing substances, designed to creep their way into the tightest possible squeezes, to dissolve the nastiest goos, to loosen the most stubborn stuck stuff, and then lubricate it all so you can turn it out with nothing more than a hand tool.

There are other liquids, sprays, goos, and ooze that one finds in the typical shop, like starting fluid (ether that ignites more easily than regular fuel and therefore gets an engine spinning when everything else fails), but use caution when considering it for your antique tractor, which probably wasn't built for ether explosions. One thing you will almost certainly find and probably need is LEAD SUBSTITUTE. For you young punks who are reading this, gasoline used to come in regular leaded and ethyl. There actually was lead in the fuel to lubricate valves in older engines. So here we are, working with those older engines in an age when leaded fuel is no longer available, There was some problem with the lead poisoning the air.

Normally old tractors will run just fine on modern unleaded gasoline (but you probably should avoid fuels with alcohol additives because they can be hard on old seals, tubes, rubber, and carburetor parts) as long as you don't run the engine hard, hot, or long. If you intend to use your tractor for real work, pulling, or even long parading, however, you might want to consider adding a lead substitute to the fuel. It is inexpensive, easy to obtain and use, and not a bad idea even for casual antique tractoring. It can't hurt, and may, after all, do some good.

In fact, I have caught Linda trying to sneak some lead substitute into my coffee some mornings.

CHAPTER 9

STAYING HAPPY AND HEALTHY IN TRACTORVILLE

I was in a hotel in Philadelphia, on about the 16th floor as I recall, taking it easy after a long day of travel, relaxing in my Roy Rogers jammies on the bed, watching some big-city television. I heard sirens in the street below, which is not unusual in the city. But they stopped somewhere close to the hotel. And then there were more sirens, and I went to the window to see what was going on. Far below on the street in front of the hotel, there were a dozen fire engines. Firemen were running around elevating ladders, running hose to hydrants, and hustling people out. Out of the hotel I was in! And then the alarms went off in the hotel.

I threw on some clothes and headed out the door. It was then and only then that I remembered that I hadn't checked that little map on the back of the door, you know, the one that says "YOU ARE HERE" and "FIRE EXITS!" Thank goodness, some of the other people on my floor obviously had taken that precaution and were headed down the hallway to the stairs and down to the lobby. We all spent that night in the Walnut Theater while the firemen put out a vent fire in the kitchen area. As I recall, the hotel went ahead and charged me for the room even though I didn't get to use it.

Maybe my reward for the trouble and cost of a room I didn't get to use was not sleeping but learning that one of the first things you should always do when you check into a hotel room is to check for emergency procedures. They are there for a reason.

It's the same with a shop. Even if you are only visiting someone else's digs, it doesn't hurt to look around for emergency equipment when you go into a shop for any time at all. And for darn sure, you want to be certain you have a full complement of emergency supplies and equipment if you ever get a shop of your own. You also want to be sure that you know where that equipment is and how to use it, and that everything is kept in operating condition. If you haven't noticed, a mechanic shop—any mechanic shop—is far more dangerous than a hotel room—any hotel room. Well, okay, maybe there are *some* hotel rooms that are more dangerous, like the ones where the sheets are on rollers, but still, you get my point.

Probably the most serious piece of emergency equipment in a shop is the FIRE EXTINGUISHER. Don't be cheap when it comes to this item. Don't settle for a bucket of water with a dead mouse floating in it or some dinky $10 extinguisher the size of a beer can that would be out of its league putting out a smoldering cigar. You want an industrial-grade extinguisher, one that is suitable for electrical and liquid fires, not just for cigar-stub-in-a-wastebasket fires. You can save yourself some bucks in this operation by buying an extinguisher that can be recharged; they are more expensive, and it's not cheap to get them refilled, but I think a good extinguisher is way too important an item for your shop to skimp on.

In fact, I'm not even satisfied with one fire extinguisher. I have one at my workbench and another by the door, close to where I do my welding. If you're dumb like I am and carelessly weld sometime while sitting down and wearing a cloth apron, you'll be glad you're close to an extinguisher. There's nothing like a crotch fire to focus one's attention on the importance of having a good fire extinguisher close at hand. Check your extinguishers annually to be sure they are charged up and ready to go.

Even if you are just visiting someone else's shop, especially if an operation starts up that involves heat or sparks like welding or grinding, just take the time to look around and spot where the extinguishers are. It doesn't take much energy and man, can that information ever come in handy.

Speaking of aprons, I do wear them in the shop (but not when washing dishes). In part, I wear them to protect my clothing so I don't have to do laundry as often and hear Linda complain about what a mess I've made of her washing machine. I wear heavy leather aprons when I am welding despite, or maybe because of, that one little mistake I made once when welding while wearing a cloth apron.

It takes some time for most men to get used to wearing a SHOP APRON. You don't want to get that caught in a revolving PTO shaft or flywheel, believe me. The hardest thing for most men to figure out when it comes to an apron is how to tie the blasted thing. I never have figured out how to tie apron strings behind my back. I have to tie the strings and then slip the apron over my head. I live in fear of pulling the wrong string behind my back some day, snarling the knot in my shop apron, and having to call the EMTs to cut me out of the dang thing.

Perhaps the most dangerous activity one does in a shop is welding. The single most important safety item when welding is appropriate eye protection, like WELDING GOGGLES or a WELDING MASK, rated for the kind of welding you will be doing. It is not advisable to have visitors in a shop when welding is going on, but if you should be the visitor, be sure you are wearing eye protection too. That arc or flame is incredibly damaging to fragile eye tissue, and the damage is permanent. Flying sparks are also a danger to eyes, and other parts of the body. Welding masks with instant darkening lenses were once way beyond the reach of the casual welder's budget, but now they are affordable and wonderfully helpful devices. If you are going to weld, be sure you have a good helmet. No, BluBlocker sunglasses won't do.

While you're at it, be sure you also have and wear gloves designed specifically for welding: heavy, insulated leather with high cuffs and no holes.

Wear a long-sleeved shirt—you'd be amazed at how "sunburned" you can get from the blazing arc of a welder! Figure that the shirt is dispensable. It won't last long, and when you throw it away, you can figure it's just that much less wear and tear on your skin.

Don't forget good shoes. High boots worn inside pant legs will save you a lot of spontaneous dancing while welding, believe me. And don't forget, this goes for you as a visitor too if you are going to be anywhere near that torch. Good footwear protects you not only from the sparks of welding, but also from dripping gobs of molten metal and even pieces of white-hot stock that drop off your work.

In fact, you should always wear sturdy *work* clothes when working (or playing) in the shop. Never wear shorts while sandblasting. Do it once and you won't need further explanation why this is a bad idea. Once you stop walking funny, you'll throw away your shorts and redecorate your torso with overalls.

GLOVES and MASKS are not just for welding. Whenever there is grinding, pounding, sanding, scraping, even rolling around under a tractor going on, the prospective patient should wear a face mask or goggles. I can't tell you how often I've been on my creeper under a tractor, working on a stuck bolt, when suddenly a big gob of greasy dirt falls off the wreckage above me and hits my face shield precisely an inch from my eyeball. Or, worse yet, the pipe wrench I left lying on top of the engine finally shakes itself loose and falls precisely where my nose would be if I weren't wearing the face shield. At moments like that, I really am grateful I took the time and trouble to pull that thing on. You'll be grateful too. Or sorry. The choice is up to you.

Another kind of mask I use a lot in my own shop is a DISPOSABLE NOSE AND MOUTH MASK to keep dust, dirt, shavings, and filings from finding their way into my breathing and digestive system. You'll want to do this too if you don't want to have PC-5, copper filing, or paint chip boogers for the next three weeks after you spend a day in the shop. Excuse the indelicacy, but that's the truth. I began using these inexpensive necessities after I started rebuilding steering wheels. I use an epoxy called PC-5 to rebuild steering wheels and then I file and grind it down to the proper profile after it hardens. No kidding, I found that for days after I worked on a steering wheel, everything I ate tasted like PC-5. And my mustache boogers were all a distinctive PC-5 gray. Hmmm, I say to myself. I bet I'm inhaling tons of this junk, and God only knows what it's doing to my lungs.

So I bought a box of disposal facemasks, put one on, and after the next couple hours working in the shop I took it off and was about to throw it away into the wood stove. I looked at it as I was about to drop it into the flames, and, holy moley! The mask's fibers where my nose and mouth had been moments before were clogged up with all manner of ugly-bugglies, which otherwise would have gone into my nose, mouth, and lungs. I now wear a facemask whenever I am working with anything that has any potential for competing with a Braunschweiger sandwich. If you are going to do any painting or sandblasting in your shop, you should consider a full-service RESPIRATOR that will filter out the finest particles.

I don't usually wear gloves to protect my hands from abrasion. My hands are never going to be used as models for fancy glove or perfume ads, believe me. I have scars on my hands from burns, scrapes, cuts, and mashings. My hands have been broken when run over by a tractor on the road, stepped on by a horse when I was thrown, hit with a hatchet when I was four years old (by me), and again just this last year. It's too late for me to wear gloves to protect my hands' beauty.

However, in my shop I do keep several packages of sturdy rubber dishwashing gloves. As I noted before, I use some pretty nasty stuff when cleaning parts: solvent, cleansers, oven cleaner, mineral spirits, and kerosene. You would be astonished to see what damage that stuff can do even to leathery old skin like mine. If those poisons won't tan your hide, and if you just go ahead and let your hands bear the brunt of the dirt and grease of mechanicking, then you're going to have to use a hand cleaner. The hand cleaner will fix you up so the love of your life won't be able to tell if you are wearing leather welding gloves or if that's just your skin.

I dread Lovely Linda reading this chapter, no kidding. She is going to look at me and snarl something about me being a hypocrite who should listen to his own good advice. Okay, so I haven't always been as careful about safety as I'm hoping you will be. And I have paid for it. No place more painfully than my ears. I am at this writing almost deaf. I attribute my tinnitus—constant and deafening ringing in my ears—to 40 years of listening to the high-pitched whining of female voices, but doctors tell me that no, the cause of my hearing problems is actually loud noises, probably from rock-and-roll and tractors.

Even though it's too late for the worst of my hearing damage, I now have ACOUSTIC EARMUFFS specifically designed to reduce noise damage (I use both earmuffs designed for shop use and some actually for shooters) hanging at several places in my shop, and I use them. (Linda won't let me wear them in the house when I'm watching hockey and she wants to explain to me why we should instead be watching yet another episode of *Friends*, however.)

No kidding, even if you are only visiting someone else's shop while a mechanic is working, take just a moment to look around for a FIRST-AID KIT. If you are building your own shop, make a good, big, industrial-grade first-aid kit a prominent part of your interior design. Or maybe two first-aid kits. I don't mean those cheesy little plastic boxes containing three Band-Aids and a Q-tip you pick up for $4.95 at K-mart. Get yourself a biggie, with lots of compresses, tape, tweezers, burn ointment, everything you hope you'll never have to use. You are not going to want to have to run to the house to find something to stop your bleeding finger or forehead while you're working, believe me. For one thing, if you do that, you are going to have to face the ridicule of, well, of, you know, the person in the house. And it just takes too much time to stop for minor wounds if you have to go somewhere else for care taking. Trust me, you are going to bleed. You are going to get burned. You *will* need first aid. As with all safety supplies and equipment, your first-aid kit is not a good place to start saving money.

You may be surprised to hear that I don't have a SMOKE DETECTOR or CARBON MONOXIDE DETECTOR in my shop. My shop is small enough that if there's a fire while I'm there, I'm going to know about it. Besides, on a normal day the air in my shop is about 9/10 smoke and dust anyway, so a detector would be going off all the time. My shop is a good 30 yards from the house, so if there's a fire or smoke when I'm not there, I wouldn't hear the bleating of a smoke alarm anyway. I suppose I should investigate some kind of warning system that would let me know in the house if there were a fire in the shop, but so far that hasn't happened.

My daughter Joyce got me a carbon monoxide detector after the little incident when I ran a tractor in the shop and damn near killed myself, but when it finally gave up the ghost, I didn't replace it. Why? Because, believe me, I will never again run an engine in my shop or any other closed area. I learned my lesson.

I do have a RADIO in my shop, not only for music and news but also for weather information. We live in an area famous for its bad weather—tornadoes, high winds, violent lightning storms, that kind of thing—and it is easy for me to become so absorbed with whatever I am doing in the shop that I forget to notice what's going on outside. So, I keep a weather warning radio too just to let me know if I should maybe head for the house to crawl under the stairs and wait out another Nebraska weather alert.

I keep wishing someone would invent a device that would warn me of the approach of a spouse, children, salesmen, tool borrowers, or thirsty-but-beer-less buddies, but so far I haven't run across anything of the sort. If you get wind of one, drop me a line and let me know. For a while I had a motion detector in my shop to let me know if burglars ever dropped by for a visit. It happens out here, especially when it comes to tools and shop equipment. But mostly it made a habit of going off when a moth or mouse passed anywhere near it, which then riled up the dogs, who woke me up in the middle of the night. Which meant I had to open the window, yell at the dogs to shut up, and then go back to sleep without so much as looking in the direction of the shop.

I have seen some shops where an INTERCOM SYSTEM terminal is a prominent feature at the workbench, even if it's nothing more than an inexpensive nursery monitor setup. This not only allows the shop worker to call for help to the house if he or she should need it, but also for someone in the house to give an occasional listen to hear for sounds of movement, whistling, hammering, cussing in the shop that indicate the mechanic of the family is in good health, or groaning, moaning, or dead silence that could indicate otherwise.

I am not very fond of a TELEPHONE in even the best of circumstances. A lot of businesses depend on folks calling on the phone; writing for a living like I do depends on folks *not* calling on the phone. When I have time to spend in my shop, the last thing in the world I want is some ding-dong calling to chat. Phone calls always seem to come at the worst possible time: You are right in the middle of welding up something or moving a motor into just the right position to slide it into the transmission, and the phone rings. Oh, man . . . So, no, I do not have a telephone in my shop and I never will. A cell phone might be handy for calling buddies for help, looking for parts, even calling for emergencies. Maybe a cell phone would be okay if I just didn't give the number out to anyone and used the shop phone only for outgoing messages. If you do have a telephone in your shop, be sure to set those first speed-dial numbers for the local EMTs and fire department. Then add your parts sources, tractor buddies, and marriage counselor. Or divorce attorney, depending on how much time or money you've been spending on your tractor or shop lately.

In our household, we sort of substitute for these kind of electronic backup systems with a personal contact arrangement. I never go to the shop without letting Linda know where I am going to be, and for how long. She checks up on me, which I appreciate, and I make a point of keeping up on my check-in schedule, which she appreciates. This may seem like overkill, but I'm not all that graceful and the shop is a dangerous place. It is rare when I come back to the house after a day in the shop without some kind of injury, however minor. A nurse was once having trouble drawing blood from me for some kind of test or another and Linda advised her, "Just hand him a butter knife and in a couple minutes you'll have more blood than you need." I would have protested, but I couldn't think of a single thing incorrect about what she said. Keeping track of my condition when I'm out in the shop seems like a good idea for us. If I can avoid it, I never work in the shop when no one else is around the place.

Nor am I a very tidy guy. You should have seen my home during my bachelor years. It wasn't pretty. My shop is a mess. But at least in my shop I try to keep things picked up, not for reasons of neatness, but for safety. Things lying around the floor of a shop are nothing more than traps for feet like mine. Falling down in a shop filled with iron tools, iron parts, iron tractors, iron motors, and iron furniture is not a good idea at all. If you're going to fall down, fall down in a house where the furniture is well padded or out in a plowed field, not in a shop. So I do what I can to keep my shop floor picked up.

I keep a good PUSH BROOM and DUST PAN close at hand for the same reasons. Linda complains bitterly when she sees a dust cloud rising from my shop door, a sign that I am once again sweeping the place out, when it would never occur to me to sweep the front room or kitchen floor in the house. She's right, but in the house cleanliness is a matter of neatness, not one of my strengths. In the shop, it's a matter of not getting hurt any worse than necessary.

I can't imagine a workbench without a good SHOP VACUUM for the same reasons. These days you can get a really good shop vac for very modest cash expenditure, and after all, a sturdy, powerful, portable vacuum is good for a lot of other jobs around a home or farm too, so this is one piece of shop equipment your Chief Financial Officer, if you catch my drift, will probably approve of with a smile. Cleanliness is next to womanliness, after all. Or something like that.

That's the end of my suggestions for shop safety equipment, but something I don't want you to forget in visiting someone else's shop or organizing your own is the LIBRARY. You're probably getting tired of my ranting about the importance of manuals, guides, catalogs, and other reference materials, but here comes that same advice again.

Don't try to re-invent the wheel or stumble through something mechanical on instinct alone. Use the good information that is so easily available to you already. My library of reference materials occupies a prominent and frequently used place in my shop. I have cut up or photocopied a lot of my reference materials and inserted the individual sheets into plastic sleeves in binders for quick, easy, sturdy, and *clean* referral in my shop. I also keep all the user's manuals and instruction booklets for my tools and equipment close at hand so I can quickly find out how to respool wire into my welder, change the disks on my angle grinder, adjust settings on the plasma cutter, that kind of thing.

Be sure you have a couple pads of paper in handy places too—mounted on the wall, at your workbench, near the door, by your library—with a pencil tied nearby on a length of string. You'll be amazed at how many things you need to remember in the shop, but are almost certain to forget before you get back to the house and take your shower—parts or tools you need, the name of the miscreant who borrowed your engine hoist, mistakes you made once and don't want to repeat any time soon again—that you'll write down, stuff in your pocket, and carry back to the house for later contemplation.

A lot of tractor guys I know also keep their stash of girlie magazines in the shop now that outhouses are no longer in fashion. I can imagine some people objecting to having such profane materials in a sanctified site like a tractor shop, but before you get all het up about this, think about something Lovely Linda once told a young woman who made the mistake of visiting my shop one day. This liberated woman took one look at the naughty girl calendars I have on my shop wall and sniffed in disgust. I tried to explain that even out in the shop I sometimes need to know what day it is, an explanation which she clearly did not accept or find amusing.

The woman turned to Linda and asked, "How can you let him put up trash like this?" Linda quietly offered up a logic that is to this very day, many years later, totally irrefutable: "Sometimes it's easier just to keep an old engine idling than to jump start it fresh every time."

Works for me.

CHAPTER 10

WELCOME TO THE CLUB

E ven though the following is absolutely critical information for the tractor and shop novice, I have tucked it back here to be sure that you have read everything else first. To my knowledge, no other guide for tractor restoration includes the following information, and yet it is perhaps the most important material you will encounter during your earliest exposure to the world of shop life, tractor work, mechanics, and tools.

Scenario: You are standing around in your uncle's shop, trying to help, trying to learn, trying not to look hopelessly stupid. He's lying on his floor creeper under the International Cub he's been working on for months. Several of his buddies, also mechanics, are sitting around, leaning on the workbench, drinking coffee, and offering suggestions. You are asking questions. Lots of questions. And everyone is being as helpful as his or her patience allows.

You: Hey, Favorite Uncle, what are you doing now? What's that black liquid running down onto your forehead? Why is the work light smoking like that? Is there anything you want me to do to help, huh?

Uncle Fred: Uh, yeah. Why don't you, er, go over to my toolbox and, uh, get me a can of headlight fluid. I think we're a little low here. And while you're at it, a can of one-D-ten-T oil. Write it down so you don't get it wrong, lil' buddy. (Thanks to Tim V. of the Yesterday's Tractors web page for this bit of drama!)

You skip off to the big red toolbox, finally able to participate in real shop work. All of your uncle's friends are chuckling and snorting as if something is really funny. Maybe they're just jealous because Uncle Fred asked you and not them.

And for the rest of your life, you are known as Little Rogie *Idiot-Oil*. It'll probably say that on your tombstone: Here lies Roger *Idiot-Oil*.

Anthropologists know this process as a "rite of passage." Whenever anyone enters into a closed, tight world of insiders like mechanics and tractor lovers, there are little tests the tyro has to face. Being sent to fetch the nonexistent tool or part is one of them. (You'll have to figure out the rest of them on your own, but if Uncle Fred tells you to wet your fingers and grab that loose spark plug wire, take my advice and think twice about it.)

In preparing this part of this book, I went to my friends at the Yesterday's Tractors web page (www.ytmag.com) and asked if anyone knew of anything I should include here. I knew there were some standard gags, but I was not at all prepared for the deluge that swept over me. I am sorry I can't credit each and every one to the contributor, but maybe it's best that they remain unnamed to avoid having potatoes stuffed into their automobile exhaust pipes or burning bags of dog poop appearing at their front doors. Here are some of the responses I got at the YT site:

Phony Tools:

- Skyhook
- Metric pliers
- Filter gauge
- Pipe stretcher
- Left-handed hammer
- Torque hammer
- High-lift dip stick
- Copper or brass magnet

Phony Parts:

- Valve bearings
- Bucket of freon (for air conditioners)
- High-speed bumper bolts
- $1/16$ scale paint (for $1/16$ scale models)
- Muffler belt
- Checkered paint
- Camo paint
- Blinker fluid
- Number 9 spots for the spot welder (also $1/16$-inch arcs)
- Quart container of neutral mixture for gearbox
- Valve cover bearings
- Bubble grease (to keep bubble in level from sticking)
- Brake (or clutch) pad lubricant
- Two spools of 1-inch pipe thread
- Concrete welding rod
- "That charged condenser lying over there on the workbench …"
- K-9P tire fluid
- Gross of spirit level bubbles 100 feet of flight line or a gallon of prop wash (for airplane mechanics), or
- Firing line (artillery or infantry) for in-flight projectile repairman …

Thermal back-draft foot-valve (tobacco can over vertical exhaust pipe. Actually, this *is* a real and important part on old tractors—the can not only keeps water out of the exhaust manifold and, therefore, the motor, when an old engine is cooling, it can draw cold air down into the head and block, warping or even breaking it, so that can slipped over the top of the exhaust stack can be a pretty important component!)

(Wow . . . this is really off the track but I just checked with my implement dealer, Steve Manzer over at Manzer Equipment in Osmond, Nebraska. I just got a brand-spanking-new AGCO ST-55 from Steve, the first new vehicle I have had since 1962, and well worth the wait. Anyway, the exhaust stack is vertical and, while slightly canted at the top, open to the skies. My pal Dick said he thinks there is some kind of new valve in there to stop moisture and cold air, but I thought I better check with Steve. Sure enough, he says yes, there *is* a hole in the bottom of the stack so water can drain, and yes, the baffles in the muffler slow cold back draft. But just in case, he says, the Prince Albert can is still standard after-manufacture equipment, even on brand-new tractors! Some technology just doesn't improve.)

Add to this list, stunts like putting black tape across a welding helmet view-port, or dropping an extra part onto a workbench where someone is rebuilding a carburetor or gearbox, and you can see that an ordinary looking workshop staffed by ordinary, everyday mechanics can be a real emotional minefield for the gullible greenhorn. Don't say I didn't warn you. And while you're at it, would you mind running into my office and getting me about 10 yards of wide margins from my word processor?

When you pass all the tests, have a couple conversations about tools and tractors, lean up against the battered fender of an ancient machine and have a cup of coffee or can of beer, and especially when some poor new greenhorn comes stumbling along and you get the nod to send him or her over to the hardware store to pick up a pound of carburetor bearing grease, you will know that you have truly entered the Grand and Glorious Fellowship of Old-Tractor Nuts. And grand and glorious it is. I have pursued a full dozen hobbies at one time or another throughout my life, everything from beekeeping to winemaking, but I have never found a pursuit so characterized by good people and good times as that which focuses on the collecting, restoration, and admiration of old tractors.

My bet is that this is just the beginning for you. Even though you might be reading this book only to learn enough so you can come closer to understanding someone else who is a certified old-tractor nut, I don't think you're going to be able to resist for long getting into it yourself. The way these things usually go, somewhere along the line, someone is going to give or sell you your own old tractor. And you're going to put together a shop. Pretty soon you'll be telling someone else about how much fun you're having banging away on old iron. I doubt that you can come this far and then simply turn around and walk away.

WHERE DO WE GO NEXT?

I have made enough of a fuss often enough in the preceding pages about the importance and value of tractor manuals, guides, and parts catalogs that I hope you have learned that lesson and know that that's the first advice I would give you again. If you are even vaguely interested in a particular make and model of tractor, get the manuals for that tractor! But if you aren't even that far along the line to Tractordom yet, I have another goofy suggestion for you.

When I first started asking friends around here about tractor mechanicking, I was a total beginner. I didn't know a rod cap from a baseball cap. But my friends were kind, patient, and gentle in their instruction and in sharing what they know and have known since they were just little kids. My buddy Dan did a very wise thing somewhere early in my learning process. It seemed a little strange, maybe even insulting at the time, but as it turned out, it was the best thing he could have done for me. He dug around in his attic and found his old high school auto shop textbooks and brought them over to me. They border on Dick-and-Jane books: "See Roger tighten the bolt! Tighten the bolt, Roger! Tighten the bolt!" But the thing is, they explain basic ideas in a basic way for a basic nudnik like me, even though I am 50 years older than the readers the book was originally intended for. (The books I have are Harold T. Glenn's *Exploring Power Mechanics* [Charles A. Bennett Co.: Peoria, 1962] and Harold T. Glenn's *Automechanics* [Bennett: Peoria, 1962]).

I would therefore suggest that you look around an old high school library, or dusty used bookstore, or eBay or Amazon.com to see if you can't find yourself an old high school mechanics text. The older they are, the closer they'll be to what you are going to be working on. You don't need a modern auto mechanics textbook with all its talk about computer analyzing, microchip technology, fuel injectors, and alternators. What you want to know about is generators, magnetos, coils, and carbs. That's what the older texts deal with.

As daunting as it may seem when you are starting from scratch, you will do just fine if you exercise the same kind of patience in assembling your shop as I recommend you use in working on your tractor. Sure, you need basic tools as described in these pages, and there are times when you need a particular tool right now. By and large, if you take it slow, bide your time, keep your eyes open, and shop around, you will accumulate what you need with minimum cost.

For example, a workbench is a fairly basic requirement in a shop, right? They aren't cheap. Well, almost no one I know who works on old tractors has a store-bought workbench in his shop. One of my workbenches is an old metal door off of a medical supply cabinet I bought when a nearby vet's hospital had a sale on furniture. Another is a bench I put together out of some old oak flooring I got out of a house that was being razed, and the third consists of a small steel table I picked up from the dumpster behind a local restaurant. I suppose it was discarded because one corner was bent down, certainly no problem for me in my shop. My friend Dick used to run an office furniture business and he recommends going to a place like this and shopping for used office desks, sturdy ones with drawers and bins. They're dirt cheap when they are old and out of style. My pal Dan has a gorgeous 20-foot-long stainless-steel workbench made from an old worktable from a school cafeteria that he bought as scrap for less than the cost of a good shirt. My buddy Dennis built his entire, huge shop—it will hold two semis at the same time—out of discarded imperfect and damaged panels from a nearby garage door manufacturer.

Get on the mailing list for a local auctioneer who works farm sales. No farmer is without a shop, and so no farm sale is without a wagon full of tools and equipment. I got some of my best industrial equipment (like my valve grinder) when I spotted a newspaper ad for an auto repair shop that was going out of business. I never could have afforded such a piece of equipment new.

Elsewhere I have mentioned websites specializing in tractor conversations. I am on three such lists. I don't very often post on the sites because there are so many other experts who know so much more than I do that I can't offer much help, but I do occasionally ask about problems I am having in my shop. It's amazing how many helpful and knowledgeable people there are out there, willing to do what they can to help a babe in the woods like me. Or you. (But do note that there are inevitably some weirdos and nut cases on sites like this too. You may find that a perfectly innocent question draws a few comments on what an idiot you are. Just ignore the nasty folks—they are usually chased away by all the good people in good time.)

There are some really nice magazines for tractor buffs, some dealing with old tractors in general (for example, *Antique Power* magazine) and some very specific (like *The Old Allis News*). These publications are not only good reading, but they offer information about services (like steering wheel restoration, for example), parts sources, and even old tractors for sale. Get hold of a catalog from MBI and take a look at the many pages devoted to books about tractors—coffee table picture books, historical surveys, tech manuals—you'll be amazed. As your interests are refined and focused, start assembling a library that addresses your specific concerns and questions. In some of my other books—written for MBI, by the way— I have insisted that a vital part of any complete shop is a good library of references and resources. Well, I think there should also be a good collection of books centering on your specific interest, whether that be motorcycles or bulldozers, Fords or Minneapolis-Molines, beside the recliner where you watch television and even beside your bed. The time will come when whatever it is you find interesting in those *Playboy* magazines will fade and carburetor adjustment will take on a new fascination for you. Believe me.

If you ask around a little, you might also find that there are organizations for tractor enthusiasts, sometimes structured as official organizations, sometimes informal gatherings of good friends who talk tractors now and then. Whenever there is a tractor show—and you'll be amazed at how many tractor shows there are in this country every year—there are also gatherings of folks with mutual interests: two-cylinder clubs, Allis enthusiasts, and people who enjoy taking their old tractors to competitive pulls. These are not only thoroughly enjoyable social gatherings, but also good opportunities to exchange information, parts, and even tractors.

My very best advice is to find yourself a couple of tractor buddies. These days some of my best friends came to me through my interest in old tractors. We throw ideas back and forth, offer advice, and generally help each other when we can. Most of all, we enjoy each other's company. Dick, Verne, Mel, Dan, Dennis, and I have had some good times with old tractors and sitting around in my shop staring at a stuck engine. We have traveled all over this country hauling tractor wreckage, and every road trip has brewed up a whole new set of stories and jokes. You'd think that finding, loading, and hauling ancient machinery would be pretty serious business, but it's mostly laughing until root beer comes out of your nose sort of stuff.

We talk about a lot of other things too—a good deal of it having nothing to do with tractors, now that I think about it. But we got to know each other first and most through old tractors. One of the main things we still have in common is old tractors. The moral of this story then is to find yourself a good tractor buddy or two. Maybe that's even more important than finding yourself a good, old tractor.

I think that's about it for what I have to offer you. I hope this has helped you in your relationship with some old-tractor nut or in getting started toward being one yourself. It's a great pursuit, with a lot of great people involved. Now you're on your way toward being one.

I hope to see you at a tractor gathering or book signing or even up at the tavern here in town sometime and maybe you can tell me some of the adventures you've had along the path to Tractorville. I can tell you this for sure: You're gonna have some.

INDEX

223